Walking With Ramona

Exploring Beverly Cleary's Portland

Laura O. Foster

Microcosm Publishing
Portland, OR

WALKING WITH RAMONA

Exploring Beverly Cleary's Portland

© *Laura O. Foster, 2016, 2019*
This edition © Microcosm Publishing, 2016, 2019

MICROCOSM PUBLISHING | 2752 N WILLIAMS AVE. PORTLAND, OR 97227

Editor: Elly Blue · **Design:** Joe Biel ·

Cover & Interior Illustrations: Meggyn Pomerleau

First Edition · October 11, 2016 · Microcosm.Pub

Second Edition · Revised · March 2019

This is Microcosm 229 · ISBN 978-1-62106-808-2

Printed on post-consumer paper with sustainable inks in the U.S.

Thanks to Louis Darling for creating Ramona's iconic look and for inspiring the illustrations in this book.

Photos by the author, except: photos on pages 24, 54, 79, 89, 114-115, courtesy of the City of Portland Archives; photos on pages 51 and 57, courtesy of the Lake Oswego Public Library; photo on page 48, courtesy of the Multnomah County Library; and photo on pages 126-27 by Kevin Foster.

If you bought this on Amazon, I'm so sorry because you could have gotten it cheaper and supported a small, independent publisher at **MICROCOSM.PUB**

Global labor conditions are bad, and our roots in industrial Cleveland in the 70s and 80s made us appreciate the need to treat workers right. Therefore, our books are MADE IN THE USA and printed on post-consumer paper.

To join the ranks of high-class stores that feature Microcosm titles, talk to your local rep: In the U.S. *Como (Atlantic), Fujii (Midwest), Travelers West (Pacific).,* ***Turnaround in Europe, and Baker & Taylor Publisher Services*** for other countries.

Library of Congress Cataloging-in-Publication Data
Names: Foster, Laura O., author.
Title: Walking with Ramona : exploring Beverly Cleary's Portland / Laura O. Foster.
Description: Portland, Oregon : Microcosm Publishing, 2016. | Series:
People's guide | Includes bibliographical references and index.
Identifiers: LCCN 2016000078 | ISBN 9781621067412 (paperback)
Subjects: LCSH: Cleary, Beverly--Childhood and youth. | Cleary,
Beverly--Homes and haunts--Oregon--Portland. | Authors, American--Homes
and haunts--Oregon--Portland. | Authors,
American--Oregon--Portland--Biography. | Literary
landmarks--Oregon--Portland. | Portland (Or.)--Intellectual life--20th
century. | Portland (Or.)--Biography. | BISAC: BIOGRAPHY & AUTOBIOGRAPHY /
Literary. | TRAVEL / Hikes & Walks. | HISTORY / United States / State &
Local / Pacific Northwest (OR, WA).
Classification: LCC PS3553.L3914 Z5915 2016 | DDC 813/.54--dc23
LC record available at http://lccn.loc.gov/2016000078

Contents

"In my books I write for the child within myself. I simply write the books I wanted to read when I used to put on my roller skates and go to the branch library."

—Beverly Cleary, in a November 16, 1961, *Oregonian* interview

1

Portland's Beverly Cleary, Ramona Quimby, and Friends

Since *Portlandia* first aired in 2011, observational comedy has had a field day with Portland's quirkiness, but Beverly Cleary was there first. Beginning with *Henry Huggins* in 1950 she's made people around the world laugh with her minutely observed scenes of life on Portland's Klickitat Street.

Not all children's books are readable by adults—even some of the ones we loved as kids. But Beverly Cleary's books are an exception, and that's perhaps why each generation finds her books fun to read: they're full of sparely crafted scenes packed with details from a kid's (or dog's) point of view. Each chapter stands alone, with satisfying endings to the quandaries and perplexities kids experience. The chapters are sometimes laugh-out-loud funny, often gently satirical, and always respectful of even the youngest child's personhood.

If you're a Portlander, her books are a treasure trove full of familiar places. This is especially true of her two autobiographies, which show one middle-class family's Portland of the 1920s and Depression-era 1930s. They're not only fascinating windows into a still recognizable Portland but also frankly show how lack of money and hope files away at a family's happiness. Beverly's struggles to stand on her own two feet were successful, of course, and her route to that success is a fascinating story for anyone who wants to follow her own path. With her books and this one, you can be in that Portland where Beverly takes the streetcar to her orthodontist downtown in the Selling Building (still there), rides a train to Camp Namanu on the Sandy River (still open), or climbs to the cave behind Multnomah Falls (off limits today).

As a child, Beverly Bunn would set a book down at the first whiff of moralizing. She decided that she'd write books to make kids laugh, with no agenda to teach them any life lessons. In her books, Henry, Beezus, Ellen, and Ramona are not just entertaining; their adventures offer glimpses into a childhood where kids had much more autonomy than they're given today. They walk alone to the market to buy horsemeat for their dog, work out major crises of which adults are oblivious, handle school crossing-guard responsibilities with dignity and authority, and mete out a harsh but effective punishment to a hair-cutting bully.

Her memories and scenes of kids operating in the sometimes confusing world of adults make Beverly Cleary's books universal and timeless. Even if you've forgotten the details of her stories, you probably remember how much you enjoyed them. Perhaps that's why when I led "Walking with Ramona," a tour of Beverly Cleary's Portland for the Multnomah County Library, we had up to 200 people appear on tour days, filling up the sidewalk along an entire city block. The demand for the tours, which were held in 2009 and 2010, has not slowed, and with this book, you have in hand your own, expanded and more detailed version of that tour.

If it's been a while since you read some of Beverly Cleary's books, do as Beverly would've done: borrow them from the library, settle next to a rain-splattered window to read, then go out, this book in hand, to experience for yourself her Portland neighborhoods, from their 1920s backstories to today's places to eat, drink and shop.

USING THIS BOOK

This book doesn't need to be read in any order. Chapter 2, Before Portlandia, gives a snapshot of the Portland that young Beverly Bunn knew in the 1920s and 1930s, a city that was nobody's idea of a vacation destination. Unlike today's Portland, it existed far from the fond gaze of the *New York Times*. Learn about horse rings, slabwood, and the beginnings of the Sunset Highway, among other historical nuggets.

The heart of the book is the Walking with Ramona tour in Chapter 3. Use the tour route to bike or walk 3.2 miles through Beverly Cleary's Hollywood and Grant Park neighborhoods. In these classic streetcar suburbs, you'll pass under Douglas firs and elms on streets lined with Craftsman bungalows and English cottage–style homes. Working class when she lived here, small homes now command high prices. On the tour, stop at places from her childhood and from scenes in her Portland books. The route is sprinkled with poetry posts and little free library stations, urban gems that Beverly never saw here, but would undoubtedly endorse. You may want to bring a book to leave at one little free library and bring a new one home. For Beverly's two homes included on the tour, respect the current owners' privacy. Don't walk up to the houses, or onto the lawns.

If you're looking for a brisk walk, the tour takes about an hour, but if you're in a sauntering/tourist mood, wanting to absorb the spirit of two of the city's most walkable neighborhoods, spend a half day or more. Combine your walk with a pint at Velo Cult Bicycle Shop, coffee at Fleur de Lis in the old library building, shopping

A poetry post near Northeast 48th Avenue and Wistaria Drive

for a locally made swimsuit at Popina Swim and Sport, treasure-hunting at Antique Alley, browsing at the Hollywood Library or the Hollywood Farmers Market, playing a game of pool at Sam's Hollywood Billiards, taking in a film at the Hollywood Theatre, and having dinner. (Chapter 5 has information about these and other places to explore; they're all on or very near the tour route.)

If you would like to take this mini vacation in Portland's Hollywood without a car, you can rent a bicycle or ride a TriMet bus or train to the neighborhood. Appendix B tells you what you need to know.

After you've explored Beverly's Portland neighborhoods, you might want to craft your own Oregon field trips, using the places listed in Chapter 4, An Oregon Checklist: Beverly and Friends Were Here. From the Roseway Theater where she watched silent movies, to the Oregon Humane Society (which cared for orphaned children when Beverly was a child), to Bridal Veil in the Columbia Gorge, the chapter offers short, fun stories about Oregon places.

BEVERLY, RAMONA, AND FRIENDS

In case it's been a while since you ran into them, here's an overview of Beverly Cleary's Portland crew:

Ramona Quimby gets top billing in this book because she's the most intriguing of all of the Portland characters. She shares many of Beverly's traits and behaviors—especially from Beverly's idyllic first six years of life on her family's Yamhill farm. Beverly, like Ramona, was small, impetuous and quick. Those six years of freedom to roam 80 acres, and of being surrounded by friends and family, etched into Beverly a joyful spirit overlain with independence and curiosity about life. This curiosity made its appearance one Thanksgiving morning in Yamhill when the blank palette of an immaculately set table with a white tablecloth inspired a preschool Beverly. She poured blue ink out, wet her hands in it and made handprints at each place setting.

Ramona has this same "What if I…" curiosity. She once squeezed all the toothpaste out of a tube to see what it would look like. "Never do that again!" her mother scolded. Ramona agreed easily: she'd done it once and saw the results. There was no need to do it twice. In an era where conventionality was the norm and children were taught never to backtalk their "betters," Beverly, even as she aged into a more cautious preteen, nurtured her inner Ramona. Throughout the places described in this book are other examples where Beverly and Ramona share a similar approach to life.

And Ramona, despite being labeled a pest, is sensitive. So was Beverly. In third grade, an adult at Gregory Heights School called Beverly a nuisance in front of her. She was humiliated and mortified, and hated when grownups talked in front of her as if she weren't there, even if it was complimentary. She was incensed at the old cliché, "Little pitchers have big ears," both for its inanity and the patronizing tone adults used when uttering it. Ramona shares this passionate personhood—she is creative and exuberant and puzzled when people call her a "show-off." She is just living boldly, with her thoughts, ideas and feelings right on the surface. Those feelings, like Beverly's, are hurt when she overhears a teacher call her a nuisance. She was just trying to break her hard-boiled egg on her forehead, like all the other kids had been doing that week. How was she to know her mother had messed up and given her an uncooked egg?

Ramona also shares Beverly's love of reading but dislike of literary analysis. Beverly hated writing book reports as both a child and college student. When Ramona is eight, her teacher announces they'll be doing "sustained silent reading" where the only objective is to read a book you like. The joy of that! The teacher comes up with a better name for sustained silent reading: DEAR, or "Drop Everything and Read." This is Ramona's idea of educational nirvana, and it becomes her favorite part of the school day. Beverly's too: in school she would hide books inside her big geography book and read what she wanted. Today, DEAR Day in public schools across the country is every April 12, Beverly Cleary's birthday.

Ramona, like just about every strong-willed kid, doesn't like to be teased, especially in clichéd ways. When Howie's Uncle Hobart teases him, in front of her, about her being Howie's girlfriend, she flatly tells Hobart, "I don't like grownups who tease." Beverly writes in her autobiography that her family's no-teasing rule was born on the Oregon Trail. In 1843, when her ancestors crossed the country in the first large wagon train to Oregon, families would spread out at night to cook and eat, so that the differences in the amount and quality of each family's meal wouldn't cause problems. The rule the pioneers followed was "No teasing, no hinting."

Anyone who found the adult world puzzling as a child can relate to Ramona. Like Ramona, Beverly questioned the status quo and the logic of things that adults do. On the first day of first grade at Fernwood School, Beverly's teacher, Miss Falb, told the class how to spell and pronounce her name, noting that the "l" was silent. If it's silent, Beverly wondered, then why is it even there?

Ramona was not intended to be a major character; she first appears as a pesky preschooler in *Henry Huggins* and grows to a fourth grader in *Ramona's World*. She was written in as sort of an afterthought, when Beverly realized that all her characters were their family's only child. But perhaps because with Ramona, Beverly allows her rebel flag to fly, Ramona became a favorite of her fans, and with subsequent books, the most nuanced of all the Portland characters.

Henry Huggins was Beverly Cleary's first character. He's an industrious boy with a creative, entrepreneurial streak. He and the dog he finds in downtown Portland, Ribsy, make a team whose adventures are sweet and funny. Though he's just an ordinary boy who is in awe of the rocket-building smarts of a neighbor boy, Henry always arrives at an inventive way to solve a problem, whether it's paying off a debt by collecting a thousand-plus earthworms, earning the right to be a paperboy, collecting the most paper in a school paper drive, or figuring out how to thwart Ramona's not so useful help in his paper route. And amazingly, all his solutions are adult-free. There is much of mid-century Portland life in the Henry Huggins series.

Ribsy is Henry's dog, but before Henry found him on the streets of downtown Portland, he had belonged to another boy. When, a year later that boy discovers Ribsy and Henry's picture in the newspaper, he comes to Klickitat Street, wanting his dog back. Searching for justice, Henry, the boy and the other kids on Klickitat come up with a creative solution for figuring out who is Ribsy's rightful owner. Even the party who didn't win had to agree it was a fair trial. This victory for sidewalk diplomacy is one that parents today, who rush in to solve kids' problems for them, should take note of. For a dog's point of view of Portland, circa 1964, the book *Ribsy* is a gem.

Beezus Quimby is Ramona's older sister and Henry's good friend. She's the classic straight man, a foil to Ramona's creativity and exuberance. She and Ramona fight often but bond one day after school when their parents are working, when the girls discover that Picky Picky, their beloved cat, has died. The sisters, trying to help keep their parents' stress level down, decide to bury the cat before their parents get home. Their problem-solving and bonding over digging the grave and creating a memorial service is realistic and touching.

Ellen Tebbits is another facet of Beverly's personality. Ellen shares Beverly's sensitivity, which grew during her Portland years under her mother's mounting criticisms and rules. Ellen worries about what adults think of her and fears that she's not making a good impression. Unlike Ramona, Ellen is quiet and an observer. Beverly came to be more quiet as she matured into adulthood and her family's tight finances and father's unhappiness cast a grey cloud over every decision and opportunity. In *A Girl from Yamhill* she wrote, "At age seven my Yamhill smile began to fade." Her mother Mable, as life in Portland became less pleasant, turned her focus on Beverly and became a helicopter parent, but without the praise and kisses.

Ellen has a best friend, **Austine Allen**, based on Beverly's best friend Claudine Klum. Austine jokes with teachers, talks back to adults and doesn't take rules too seriously. Ellen is in awe of her friend's bravery. Beverly liked that about Claudine and also was fond of Claudine's mother, who joked and laughed with her daughter and her friends. People smiled in Beverly's home, she wrote, but no one laughed out loud.

Otis Spofford is one of those boys who inhabit every classroom: a boy who works harder to get a laugh than on the work at hand. He lets his guard down when he takes his shoes off one day in Laurelwood Park and gets his comeuppance, courtesy of Ellen Tebbits. The lake where it happens is in Portland's Laurelhurst Park.

Howie Kemp. He's Ramona's partner in play. In a game called brick factory, Ramona and Howie smash old bricks into dust. Howie is a lot like Beverly's real life cousin Winston: slow-moving, good natured and deliberate. As preschoolers in Yamhill, Beverly and Winston smashed bricks together, too. Winston had a younger sister named Donna. Howie has a younger sister named Willa Jean who, as Ramona ages, inherits the mantle of the neighborhood pest but without Ramona's inventiveness.

Near Beverly's 37th Avenue home: Northeast Stanton Street and Wistaria Drive, at the base of Alameda Ridge

MILESTONES IN BEVERLY BUNN CLEARY'S LIFE

1916 Born in McMinnville, Oregon, to Chester Lloyd Bunn and Mable Atlee Bunn

1922 Bunn family moves to Portland from the family farm because agricultural commodity prices are too low to support them

1934 Graduates from Grant High School

1934 Attends Chaffey College, a junior college in Ontario, California

1938 Graduates from University of California, Berkeley, with a B.A. in English

1939 Graduates from the School of Librarianship, University of Washington, Seattle, with a specialty in children's literature

1939 Works in Yakima, Washington as a children's librarian

1940 Marries Clarence Cleary of Sacramento and moves to Berkeley

1948 Begins writing her first children's book after several years working in a bookstore

1950 *Henry Huggins*, her first book, is published

1955 Twins, Malcolm and Maryanne, are born

1978 Receives Newberry Honor for *Ramona and Her Father*

1981 Receives National Book Award for *Ramona and Her Mother*

1982 Receives Newberry Honor for *Ramona Quimby, Age 8*

1984 Receives Newberry Award for *Dear Mr. Henshaw*

1995 Dedicates, with Clarence, the Beverly Cleary Sculpture Garden in Portland

2000 Named a Library of Congress Living Legend in the Writers and Artists category

2003 Receives the National Medal of Arts

2015 Over 91 million books sold, worldwide

2016 Beverly celebrates her 100th birthday. Oregon Public Broadcasting airs TV special *Discovering Beverly Cleary*.

2

Before Portlandia:
Beverly Cleary's Portland
of the 1920s and 1930s

For Beverly Cleary's family in the 1920s and 1930s, Portland was not a place where local foods were celebrated and civic weirdness was an asset. The air often had, as Beverly remembered, the "rotten cabbage" smell of the paper mill in Camas, Washington, which turned wood pulp into newsprint for the *Oregonian*. Manufacturing was a big part of the city, and the Willamette River was lined with mills, working docks, warehouses and factories. Clean air and water regulations did not yet exist. Untreated sewage flowed into the Willamette and the Columbia Slough. The Willamette, from Eugene to its mouth, was referred to as an open sewer. Downtown Portland flooded seasonally until the Harbor Wall was completed in 1929, when Beverly turned 13.

STREETCAR SUBURBS

On the east side of the city, there was plentiful, relatively flat ground compared to the west side, where Portland had been founded. Once bridges began crossing the Willamette River in the late 1800s, followed by streetcars, the east side began to turn from farms and woods to neighborhoods, initially called streetcar suburbs. After Portland's 1905 World's Fair, the city's population took a huge leap and new subdivisions were built to meet the demand. Rose City Park— which today's Hollywood was part of—was platted (mapped out) in 1907, and was served by a new streetcar line on Sandy Boulevard. By 1922, when Beverly and her family moved here, Rose City Park and nearby neighborhoods continued to fill in, as vacant lots turned into tidy yards sprouting Craftsman bungalows and English cottage–style homes. Beverly's dad, Lloyd, rode the Sandy Boulevard streetcar to work every day in downtown Portland.

Streetcar use reached its peak in the 1920s, then declined because of automobiles. Initially a rich man's toy, cars became more affordable, changing the face of urban neighborhoods as garages were added to 50-by-100-foot lots and concrete driveways poured to accommodate a family's new purchase. Most old streetcar routes are now TriMet bus lines.

SLABWOOD AND HORSE RINGS

Portland homes were heated by wood or coal. A common sight was a cord of wood dumped in the parking strip between a home's sidewalk and the street, to be stacked until a crew came to cut the wood into furnace-size lengths. It'd then be loaded into the basement, to feed the furnace throughout the winter. Beverly's loathsome suitor, Gerhart, who was from California, ridiculed Oregonians for this rustic practice. Beverly referred to it as slabwood, which is the name—once a slur but now a badge of authenticity—for the Northwest Portland neighborhood called Slabtown. Slabwood had the bark left on; it was cheaper than clean cordwood, with bark removed. Perhaps due to her family's tight budget, they had slabwood, not cordwood, delivered to their home.

During Beverly's childhood, she would have seen milk, ice, wood, and groceries delivered by horse-drawn wagon. One of the things Beverly loved about her home on 37th Street (as it was then known—see "What Beverly Saw" on page 22) was the tiny door on the side of the house, where the milkman placed the week's delivery of milk, cream, butter, and ice cream.

Horse rings for tying up horses are still seen throughout old Portland neighborhoods. They're embedded in concrete curbs poured in the first decades of the 1900s. You'll see some in the Walking with Ramona tour in Chapter 3. Gasoline-powered trucks began replacing horses from the 1920s on, but deliveries by horse-drawn

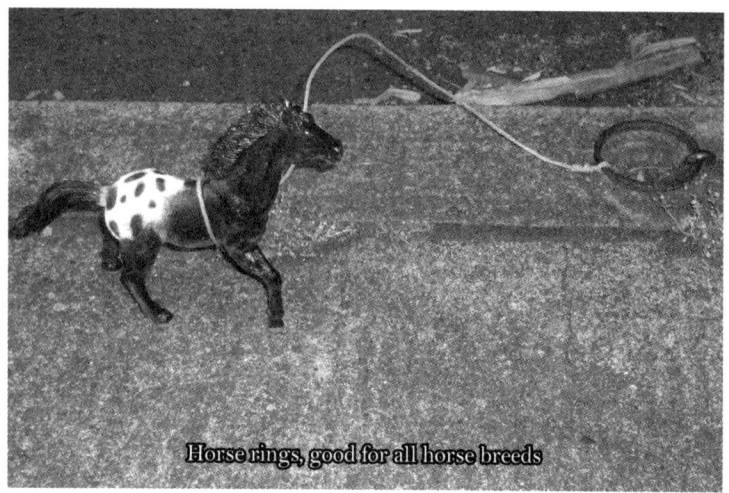
Horse rings, good for all horse breeds

wagon existed until about the start of World War II. The rings are now one of the city's urban treasures, often found with toy horses or dinosaurs tied to them, and toy boats in the fall, when street drains clog with leaves.

SILENT MOVIES AND OREGON EXPLORING

As a child in Portland, Beverly walked to movies at the Roseway and Hollywood theaters. As a third grader, she learned to read fast by reading titles as they flashed up on the screen during silent movies. When she got a little older, she rode the streetcar "overtown" into downtown Portland for her orthodontist appointments, took a chartered train to summer camp at Camp Namanu along the Sandy River, and spent two weeks at Rockaway Beach one summer. The beach visit was a prescription given by the family doctor as a restorative cure after Beverly had suffered several bouts of illness. She and her parents took the train to the coast, a travel option that now seems fantastic, but no longer exists. There was no highway from Portland to the beach at the time (except Route 30 to Astoria). The Wolf Creek Highway began construction in 1933 as a Depression work relief project. It's now called the Sunset Highway or U.S. 26.

Beverly loved visiting the tiny town of Banks, in the northern Tualatin Valley—today a terminus of the Banks to Vernonia State Trail, a bike and pedestrian trail created on an old rail line. A passenger train once ran from Portland to Banks. There, at her grandparents' general store, she watched as they bought goods for the store from "drummers," as traveling salesmen were then called. In high school, wanting to earn her own spending money, she asked her parents if she could spend part of the summer with her grandparents in Banks, cutting sword ferns in the woods to send back to florists in New York City. They said no. Other farm work that city kids often did was picking strawberries, an Oregon tradition until child labor laws wiped that out. Beverly's mom, perhaps because she hated her years of farm work, never allowed her daughter to do it.

One thing that hasn't changed since Beverly's childhood is Portlanders' love for leaving town to explore the mountains, gorge and coast. After selling their Yamhill farm in 1927, the Bunns bought a Model A Chevrolet and drove out the Columbia River Highway, a twisty road that Beverly noted Oregonians never got carsick on, because they stopped to admire every waterfall along the way. Before Timberline Lodge was built, they drove up to Mount Hood to look down into the Willamette Valley from above the timberline; nearby, a caged bear drank orange soda from a bottle. They drove out to Prineville to see Beverly's Aunt Dora who taught in a one-room school, and into the high desert south of The Dalles. She spent happy times with friends on the Zigzag River on Mount Hood, and along the Pudding River near Canby. They did not have the Chevrolet for very long; as the Depression deepened, Beverly's dad lost his job and they sold the car.

Depression Hardships

For Beverly, her Portland life, from ages 6 to 18, was a chapter when there was never enough money and family life grew increasingly stressful. Her dad, Lloyd Bunn, was a reluctant Portlander, better suited by skill and temperament to be a farmer. His unhappiness at work, and then, later at being unemployed, sometimes erupted into rages or simmered during bouts of depression. Her mother, Mable Bunn, was an intelligent woman constrained by a "what will the neighbors think" mindset and the lack of work opportunities for married women in that era. The Bunns loved their only daughter dearly, but their household was one in which laughter was seldom heard. The days on the Yamhill farm retreated into a happier past as the years in Portland piled up.

Perhaps because she'd known both freedom and constraints as a child, Beverly Bunn Cleary grew up to be fun-loving, sensitive, and an observer of human quirks. As she matured into a teen during the hardest years of the Great Depression, she was filled with an ambition to follow her own path and stand on her own two feet— like her pioneer forebears who had walked the Oregon Trail and floated the Columbia River to arrive in the Willamette Valley in 1843. Through the success of her books she has done exactly that.

What Beverly Saw: Portland's Changing Address System

It's easy to navigate around Portland, thanks to a logical and easy-to-remember address system. The city has four quadrants—Northeast, Southeast, Southwest and Northwest—that neatly fit the city's geography. Two axes separate the quadrants: the Willamette River and Burnside Street. The Willamette is the north-south axis: it flows north through the city, forming the boundary of the east and west sides of town. Burnside Street, the longest street in town, is the east-west axis. It divides the city north and south.

There's also a fifth quadrant, North Portland, that isn't as neat a fit, because the river takes a sharp turn north of downtown. Beginning at Williams Avenue and running northwest from there, this quadrant is a peninsula, bordered by the Willamette and Columbia rivers. Throughout the city, north-south roads are called avenues; east-west roads are called streets. Even-numbered addresses are on the south or east sides of roads; odd numbers are on the west or north sides.

For example, if you know the address of Beverly's home at 2924 NE 37th Avenue, you can figure out that it's a north-south road, it's 29 blocks north of Burnside Street, 37 blocks east of the Willamette River, and is on the east side of the street. For a non-numbered street name it's still pretty easy: a business at 1214 SE Tacoma Street is on an east-west running street, 12 blocks east of the Willamette River. It's south of Burnside, and on the south side of the street. The street name, however, doesn't tell you how far north or south of Burnside it is, unless it's part of the alphabetized streets (Ankeny, Burnside and on through the alphabet to York), most of which are on the west side of the Willamette.

When Beverly Cleary was a girl, this elegant system wasn't yet in place. Today, Oregon has a national reputation for urban planning, with our land use laws and Urban Growth Boundary, but that wasn't the case during her childhood. By the 1920s, 50 years of urban growth meant that street names and numbers followed no unifying pattern. When nearby towns such as Sellwood, Linnton and Albina had become Portland neighborhoods, they kept their street names and numbers, even if they duplicated existing street names. By 1920, nearly everyone in town had a story of a frustrating address odyssey, and the *Oregonian* complained, "Three business firms on Sixth Street carry the number '47' over their doors."

It took until 1930 for a solution. That year, the city engineer and postmaster solved the problem by borrowing a system from Philadelphia and an address tile design from Milwaukee, Wisconsin. The City contracted with Gladding, McBean Company, a tile manufacturer in Lincoln, California. It stopped its work making roof tiles for Stanford University long enough to manufacture 396,000 porcelain number tiles for Portland. The tiles have a white background with black numerals.

It was a project well-timed with the Great Depression, which robbed many men of their jobs. Installing the new tiles on every home and business in town kept teams of men employed from 1931 to 1933. The teams pushed carts loaded with tile numbers along city

In this 1933 photo, crews are installing a new address on a Portland home. The old address is still above the door. Carts for the address tiles were fashioned out of wood and bike tires.

sidewalks. One man stood at the end of a block, assigning numbers. Another pulled tiles from the cart and arranged them into a metal frame. Others installed them. Each night, carts were stowed in the closest firehouse and the men walked home, grateful for the few dollars earned that day.

The first number went up at 7340 N Philadelphia Avenue, on the Peninsula National Bank Building near the St. Johns Bridge. Twenty-two months later, new addresses were in place at 93,596 locations. 30,000 digits remained. So, for decades, new homeowners were handed a set of address tiles with their construction permit. Though the city no longer gives out the tiles, you can find originals at architectural salvage stores, and new ones at some local retailers such as Schoolhouse Electric.

You can still find remnants of the old system if you know where to look. In neighborhoods with Queen Anne-style homes, look at the transom windows over front doors. Sometimes the old number is still there, etched in clear glass or outlined in stained glass. If you see a sidewalk stamped with the wrong street name, that's a remnant, too. And sometimes there'll be a numbered street called "Place" instead of Avenue—those are almost always short north-south streets that had a different name pre-1931. To keep the numbers aligned, these streets had to be given a number/name combo that wouldn't throw everything off. Northeast 35th Place, north of Grant Park, is an example. It used to be called Marguerite Street. When curbs have to be replaced to make the sidewalks accessible, the City honors the old street name and stamps it into the new curb.

On the Chapter 3 walking tour, the old tiles still hang from Beverly's 37th Avenue home. They were installed during the years she lived there.

COFFEE CAN STILTS ACTIVITY

Beverly and her friends built themselves stilts out of two-pound coffee cans, and clumped down Portland's sidewalks. It's never too soon to join the DIY crowd, and this is a perfect 1920s-era project a kid can do.

FOR EACH PAIR OF STILTS YOU'LL NEED

- Two large empty metal cans. Really big ones, like a six-pound, six-ounce tomato can from a store like Cash and Carry mean small-footed kids can go barefoot atop the can. Smaller 28-ounce cans work fine too, but feet will stick over the can's ridgy edge, so shoes will be needed.

- A big fat nail (like a drywall nail) and hammer to drive holes through the cans

- Measuring tape

- Heavy jute or twine

- Optional decorating supplies: Two lengths of paper, cut to the height and diameter of each can, plus paints, markers or crayons, and glue to stick the paper to the can

MAKE YOUR STILTS

1. The open ends of the cans will be the bottom of the stilts. Wrap the measuring tape around the first can, about 1 inch below the top. Make a mark on the can at both the beginning and halfway points of your measuring tape. Pound in a nail at your first mark. Pull the nail out to leave a hole. Pound the nail in at the other mark and pull it out. Do the same thing for the second can.

2. Optional: Decorate the paper then glue it to the cans. Use the nail to poke through the paper at the holes you made in Step 1, so you can thread the twine through the holes in the next step.

3. Make the handles: Push the twine through the holes in the first can, doubling it if it's thin. It may help to wrap a bit of tape around the end of the twine so it's less frayed and easier to push through the holes. Once it's through both holes, cut the twine long enough so you can grab the handles with fully extended arms. Tie off the twine and knot it a few times. Repeat for the other can.

4. Step up on your stilts and clump down the sidewalk, making as much noise as possible. Practice every day so you can be in the next Junior Rose Festival Parade.

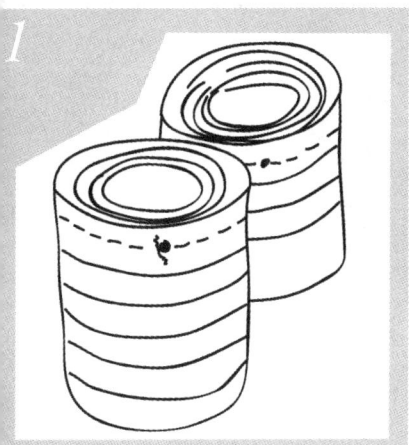

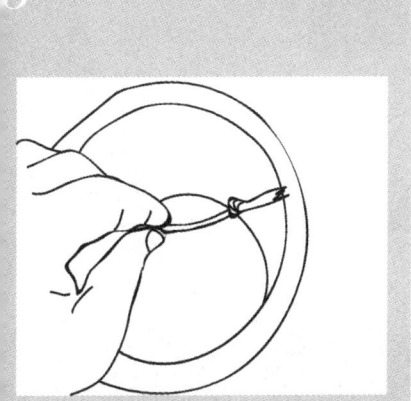

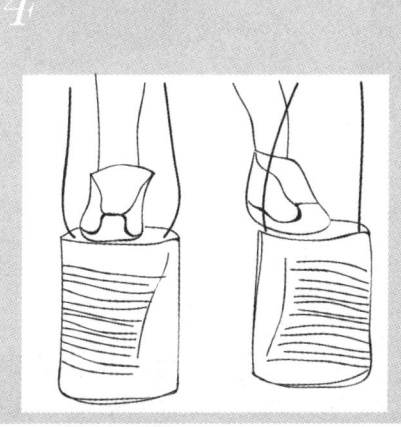

3

Walking (or Biking) with Ramona: A Neighborhood Tour of Hollywood and Grant Park

Beverly Cleary's neighborhoods, Grant Park and Hollywood, are two of Portland's many urban gems—the kind of neighborhoods you settle into, and which become your small town within the big city—where every trip to the grocery store, library, park, or gym has you bumping into friends or acquaintances. It's been that way since the days when the homes were new, cars were few, and kids built stilts out of two-pound coffee cans and twine.

On this walk you'll discover the homes Beverly lived in, the park she dug night crawlers in, schools she wrote her first essays in, sidewalks she roller-skated on, and neighborhood places she made famous in her books for children.

To get a stronger sense of Beverly's Portland, take public transit to the start. Back when she was an Oregonian, the city had a dense weave of streetcar tracks connecting all neighborhoods to downtown, and also to interurban rail lines that could take you just

A Hollywood Craftsman bungalow

about anywhere, from ocean beaches to a salmon stream in Mount Hood's foothills. You could ride the streetcar to work, to your dentist's office or to an amusement park on the river.

Today, many of TriMet's bus lines follow the same routes as the streetcars. Buses are equipped to carry bikes. See Appendix B for which bus or light rail train to take. If you drive, there's free parking along Northeast 33rd Avenue and the side streets west of it.

UPFRONT INFO

Find public restrooms in the Hollywood Library, which is about halfway through the route. Along the route you'll also find cafes or stores with restrooms for customers. Bring money and allow time not just to walk or bike through the neighborhood but also to have a meal, a beer or coffee, shop for a Portland-made swimsuit, play a game of pool, or go to an independent film at the neighborhood's eponym, the Hollywood Theatre.

The walk is about 3 miles, mostly flat, and on sidewalks and park paths. The route travels through neighborhoods, a 20-acre park, and Hollywood's streetcar-era commercial district. There's one short staircase at the start that could be circumvented, and one hill up to Klickitat Street on Alameda Ridge—a 4-mile-long deposit of gravel that sheltered the Bunns' home from winter's east winds. Nearby is a long, optional staircase up to the top of the ridge, where views are good.

For businesses, shown in boldface, find hours and other details in Chapter 5.

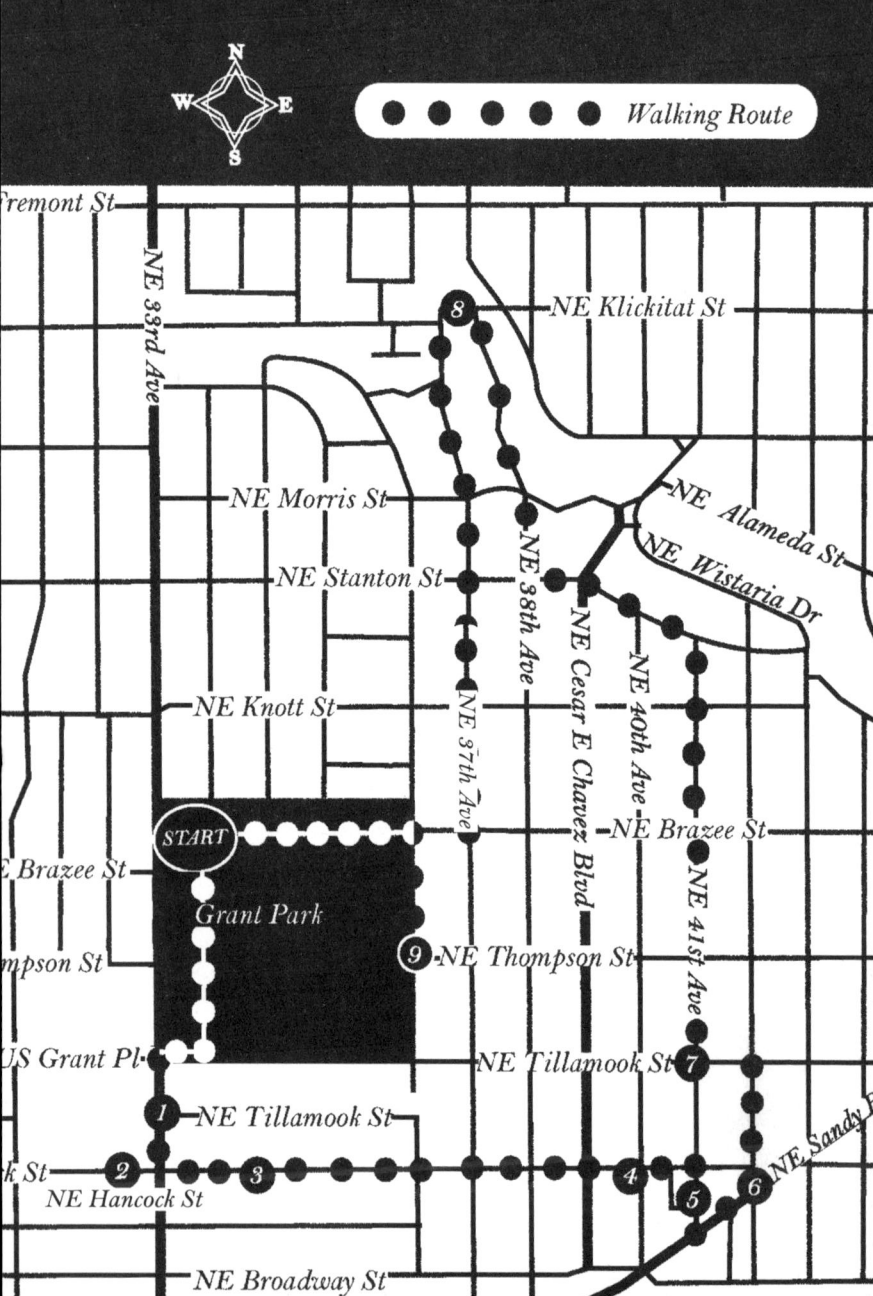

Grant Park **Start**

BEGIN AT NORTHEAST 33RD AVENUE AND BRAZEE STREET, ON THE WEST EDGE OF GRANT PARK. CLIMB THE ELEVEN STEPS INTO THE PARK. THEY LEAD TO A PATH. Immediately on the right is a giant sequoia, probably planted when the park was new in 1922. It's not a tree native to Oregon, but to California's western Sierra Nevada. It's the largest tree species in the world by volume, though not the tallest (that'd be the coast redwood, a relative of this tree). The first giant sequoias came to Oregon as tiny cones in the saddlebags of a Washington County nurseryman, John Porter. He'd ridden his horse to California in the 1850s to search for gold. He found these instead.

This beautiful tree is a fine introduction to Grant Park. In the Pacific Northwest you can often find a city park by looking for a tall stand of evergreens, usually Douglas firs, sticking up above the surrounding urban landscape. Grant Park, from here and running east along the high school, is no exception. It's one of Portland's many classic parks from the early twentieth century.

FROM THE GIANT SEQUOIA, TURN LEFT AT THE FIRST JUNCTION AND WALK TO THE BEVERLY CLEARY SCULPTURE GARDEN. Dedicated in 1995 with Beverly and Clarence Cleary present, the sculptures are the work of Portland artist Lee Hunt, who sculpted them in clay and then cast them in bronze. The fountains here turn on in summer and replace the old circular wading pool that generations of Portland parents sat around, watching their toddlers splash. It sits, unused now and unfilled (except when leaves clog the drain in late fall) just east of the sculptures.

The boy sculpture is Henry Huggins, Beverly's first fictional character, from 1950's *Henry Huggins*. He's ready for action, with his

Henry Huggins

Ribsy

baseball in hand. In his jacket he's got a snack for later. It's presumably the same jacket he hid four squirming kittens in when he went to Knott Street to ask Mr. Capper for a paperboy job.

Next is Henry's dog Ribsy, a city mutt with a great love for his boy. Beverly created him as the antithesis of all the noble, smooth-coated dogs like Lassie she'd read about as a kid. He's a bit big here—too big to be the dog that Henry found downtown, squashed into a cardboard box, and tried to sneak home on a bus. But perhaps that's intentional: this Ribsy is big enough to be ridden. His shiny back and ears polished by thousands of tiny hands speak to his popularity. When she wrote her first draft of *Henry Huggins* in Oakland, California, Beverly called her manuscript "Spareribs and Henry." Her night's dinner, waiting in her fridge, inspired the name. Her editor, who loved the book on first read, suggested Beverly consider a better name for the dog, and so "Ribsy" was born. And it was a name that fit because when Henry found him, all his ribs were showing.

The third statue is Ramona Quimby who, during the Ramona series, grows from a tantrum-throwing preschooler who rules Beezus with her volatility to a curious, creative and sensitive grade-schooler. Today, her parents would have Ramona transferred into Buckman and da Vinci, Portland's arts-oriented public schools. But in the books, while amused by Ramona, Dorothy and Robert Quimby are usually tired. Like most parents in earlier eras, they didn't get as involved in the day-to-day goings on of their kids. Sometimes her dad is depressed and out of work—like Beverly's own dad once was—and in one book he enrolls at Portland State to get a teaching degree. Her mom works in a doctor's office to pay the mortgage on a home addition. Because money was tight, Ramona always wears hand-me-downs. Here her raincoat is many sizes too big, with cuffs rolled several times to fit. It will last her for years.

Grant Bowl, Tillamook Street, and Ramona's muddy parking lot ❶

FROM THE SCULPTURES, WALK SOUTH. The trees on your left with the globby lumps in their trunks are London planetrees. They're messy trees but resilient—kind of like Ramona. The tree's name was born because of air pollution in London, England. During the Industrial Revolution and for years afterward as residents heated their homes with coal, the air was often a dark stew of pollutants. When it got extremely bad, people had to feel their way home by clutching railings along the sidewalks. Visibility during the killer fog of 1952 dropped to one foot. This tree was one of the few that could survive, and so it was widely planted there.

FOLLOW THE DIRT PATH SOUTH ALONG THE TOP OF THE SUNKEN GRANT HIGH TRACK AND FIELD. When Beverly was in eighth grade, Portland Public Schools had its physical education teachers instruct their

Ramona

students to perform an identical, sequenced set of calisthenics. In spring Beverly joined her Fernwood School classmates and hundreds of other Portland school kids here in what she called the Grant Bowl, in a precision calisthenics drill not unlike a Hitler Youth assembly. In 2013, the renovated track and field were dedicated as the Mark Cotton Field, in honor of Grant High's track and cross-country coach, who coached from 1965 to 1990. The artificial turf replaced grass, which is not a great field surface for Portland's long wet season. Nike, with its hometown next door to Portland in Beaverton, Oregon, gave $350,000 toward the $2 million renovation. Across the street as you walk along the track are charming English cottage-style homes.

AT THE SOUTH END OF THE TRACK, LEAVE GRANT PARK AND WALK TO THE CORNER OF 33RD AVENUE AND U.S. GRANT PLACE. CONTINUE SOUTH (LEFT) ON 33RD. CROSS TILLAMOOK STREET. In *Ellen Tebbits* and *Otis Spofford*, Ellen and her best friend Austine Allen live on Tillamook Street. The Tillamook, also known as the Nehalem, are Native Americans from the Oregon Coast. It's also been spelled *Kilamox* and *Killamuck*.

AT THE NEXT STREET, HANCOCK, CROSS 33RD AT THE TRAFFIC LIGHT. Ahead is the old Fernwood Grammar School, with a more modern

front door on its east side. While you're waiting to cross, consider that this is the exact corner where kindergartener Ramona Quimby waited while Henry Huggins, a fourth-grader, managed traffic one rainy day. She looked over to the new grocery store being built across from the school (at the site of today's **QFC**) and saw how delicious the mud was. How wonderful it'd be to squish through it with her new red rain boots! With the rain chasing the contractors off the job for the day, when Henry began ushering kids across the street, Ramona bolted over and plunged into the mud, ignoring Henry's yells to come back. She got stuck, and Henry had to come over and carry her out—leaving one precious boot behind. To Henry's great embarrassment, kids hung out the school windows and cheered and jeered at them both.

When Beverly Bunn went to school at Fernwood, the corner grocery was Abendroth's. Carl Abendroth was the sort of multi-preneurial Portlander you often meet these days: he was a professional bicycle racer, a printer at times, an acrobat on the Orpheum Vaudeville circuit, and a grocery store owner. His brother Adolph ran the business after Carl's death in 1925 until 1929—years Beverly was at school here. The store was also called the Fernwood Grocery.

In *A Girl from Yamhill*, Beverly wrote that Abendroth's once sponsored a contest for Fernwood School students. The winner of the best animal essay would win $2. She chose to write about Oregon's state animal, the beaver. Her essay won, partly because she was already a good writer, but more so because she was the only student who submitted one. What she said about that was, "Try! Others will talk about writing but may never get around to trying."

After Abendroth's, the market expanded and was a Kienow's Grocery until 1999. QFC moved in then.

Beverly Cleary School, Fernwood Campus 2

Once across 33rd Avenue, you're at Beverly's school, Fernwood Grammar School. It's now Beverly Cleary School, Fernwood Campus. **IF YOU WANT A PICTURE, WALK TO THE SCHOOL'S EAST ENTRANCE** where a gorgeous mosaic on the red brick wall makes a great backdrop.

WALK A HALF BLOCK WEST ON HANCOCK STREET TO THE RAISED LAWN IN FRONT OF THE OLDEST SECTION OF THE SCHOOL. Through the green doors with the arch over them, now sidelined by the more modern entrance, young Beverly Bunn stepped to start her school career.

This center part of the building and one of the two flanking sections were built in 1911 when the neighborhood was first platted. Many Portland schools in that era were built in modular units, with new sections added as neighborhoods were built up and the number of students increased. Later sections, including an auditorium (not visible here) were added to Fernwood in 1924.

Beverly went to school here from first to eighth grade (except for third grade, when she went to Gregory Heights). Before she started school, she had loved books because her mother read to her and her dad every night: myths, fairy tales, and travel books. Mable had started the town's first library in the year before they left Yamhill, and Beverly, whose first reading material had been a booklet of Jell-O recipes, was thrilled when crates of books arrived from the Oregon State Library in Salem. Like Ramona with her first library book, Beverly found a book that spoke to her, *More English Fairy Tales.* Her mother had to pry it from her hands at night. She loved a story in it, "The Little Hobyahs," that would never be read to a preschooler today. In it, the nighttime comings of the nasty, ill-intentioned Hobyahs wake a family's dog, who barks to alert his owner. Over the course of

many evenings, the owner, angry with the dog for interrupting his sleep, cuts off parts of the dog's anatomy, to punish him for barking.

But in her first few years here at Fernwood, Beverly hated reading. The books, she later wrote, were boring, with no conflict, no story, just lines like "See Spot run." No way could that compete with the shivery thrills delivered by the little Hobyahs. After missing weeks of school when she got sick with smallpox, Beverly was put in the low reading group and felt ashamed. By third grade, however, she'd found books that held her interest and she had become a reader for life.

At Fernwood, Beverly loved to sing the dawnzer song with her class: "O say can you see, by the dawnzer's lee light?" In *Ramona the Pest*, Ramona loves to sing the dawnzer song at her school, Glenwood.

In 1927 when Beverly was 11, a boys-eating-garlic fad swept through Fernwood. This was not the Italian section of Portland, and people who weren't from Mediterranean cultures weren't cooking with garlic back then. The unfamiliar smell emanating from the mouth-breathing boys made girls shriek and hold their noses. The principal ended the fad: he walked across the street to Abendroth's and bought a dollar's worth of garlic. He had the garlic-eaters sit in his office and eat it until it was gone. Beverly notes succinctly, "A dollar bought a lot of garlic in those days." She repurposed parts of this story in *Otis Spofford*.

In seventh grade at Fernwood, Beverly's teacher praised her writing: "When Beverly grows up, she should write children's books." Beverly had written her story while the rain beat against the windows, and she said later that she has always had the urge to write when it rained.

Beverly's third Portland home: 3340 NE Hancock St. **3**

FROM THE SCHOOL, GO BACK TO NORTHEAST 33RD AVENUE AND HANCOCK STREET, CROSS 33RD, AND WALK EAST ON HANCOCK, where it immediately becomes quiet residential. Here, about half a block from Fernwood, Beverly Bunn lived from fourth to seventh grade. The neighborhood was full of young families, a real bonus to only-child Beverly. In *A Girl from Yamhill*, she recalls children huddling together on porches to listen through open windows as comedy shows played on the radio. Henry Huggins was inspired by the boys she knew on Hancock Street. In her fiction, the street became Klickitat Street. The real Klickitat Street comes up later in this tour.

Most homes in this neighborhood were built between 1905 and 1930. Beverly would've heard the sound of carpenters' hammers pounding together walls and roofs as she and her friends played on the street. As in many old Portland middle class neighborhoods, some homes were mail-ordered from a catalog. A home would arrive in up to 30,000 pieces via boxcars at the nearest rail yard. The parts were trucked to the building lot and the home was put together. Everything you'd need to build a house was included: lumber, windows, hinges, doors, lights.

The Hancock Street house was her family's third and last rental home in Portland. First they had lived at 28th and Halsey during her first and second grade years. Then, because her mom felt the neighborhood was not safe near Sullivan's Gulch, they moved to 77th near Fremont Street for third grade. In that year she attended Gregory Heights Elementary. (See Chapter 4 for more on those two homes.) The Bunns returned to this neighborhood the summer before Beverly's fourth grade year.

The home at 3340 Hancock Street was built in 1910. Its address then was 1014 Hancock Street. (See Chapter 2 for the story of

Beverly's home on Hancock Street

What Beverly saw while doing needlework on her Hancock Street porch

Portland's great street renaming and renumbering.) The concrete street and many of the sidewalk segments have not changed since Beverly walked, biked, and roller-skated along them. She remembers Hancock Street as tree-lined, and it still is, though probably only one of today's street trees remains from her childhood: an enormous

European white elm at 3331, almost directly across from her home's front porch.

As an only child, Beverly loved playing with other kids, and her happy memories on this block were a foundation for her books. However, it was in this house that Beverly remembers a shadow of sorrow began to fall across her family. Her dad, Lloyd, was raised on his family's Yamhill farm and his education had stopped after tenth grade. He had always intended to farm, but poor crop prices had forced the family off the farm in 1922. He hated his jobs standing as a watchman in Portland banks and became increasingly depressed, even falling into rages at times. Beverly's mom Mable, trying to help with finances, took a job selling *McCall's* magazine subscriptions from home. Beverly escaped her mother's repetitive telephone sales pitch by walking or roller skating to the library seven blocks east on Hancock or sitting on the home's front porch doing needlework.

Rose City Park branch library ④

FROM BEVERLY'S HANCOCK STREET HOME, WALK EAST ON PEACEFUL HANCOCK PAST OLD BUNGALOWS. At 36th Avenue the homes get larger and more Craftsmanlike in style. At César E. Chávez (39th), you may want to detour half a block to the right for a stop at **BASKIN ROBBINS, THE HOBBY SMITH** or **SPARK ARTS CENTER.**

BACK ON HANCOCK, STOP AT 40TH AVENUE, AT FLEUR DE LIS BAKERY AND CAFÉ. It's inside the second library building to have occupied this site. The red brick Georgian-style library Beverly used—called the Rose City Park branch library—was torn down in 1959 and replaced with this space-age structure (check out the cone-shaped roof), which was called the Hollywood Library from 1959 to 2002. Beverly's many happy hours reading in the old library's wicker chairs triggered her career choice. With her teacher's encouragement, she decided in seventh grade that when she grew up she would write children's books. Her mother Mable, ever practical and with no praise given, simply said, "If you want to be a writer you need a career with steady income." So Beverly decided then and there to become a librarian.

The current Hollywood Library is seen later in the route. When Beverly lived here, the area around this library was part of the Rose City Park neighborhood so when the library opened in 1926 it took that name. The Hollywood Theatre opened that year too. Over time, as it became the district's most prominent business, the Hollywood name started accruing to the entire district.

In *Beezus and Ramona,* the library is called the Glenwood Branch Library. It is here, when Ramona is getting her first library card, that the librarian requests her father's occupation, asking, "What does your father do?" Her answer: "He mows the lawn." The inspiration for this scene came from Beverly's year as a children's librarian in Yakima, Washington. Listing the father's occupation was part of a child's library card application. When one child was asked what his father did, he answered, "He types." That child's dad was a lawyer.

ACROSS 40TH AVENUE from the old library are the London Plaza Apartments. They were built in 1926 as the Rose City Plaza Apartments when Beverly was 10. Near the Sandy Boulevard streetcar, they are typical of streetcar-era apartment buildings that went up all over Portland, even as the streetcar was being chased off the road by the automobile.

Beverly would've walked by the apartments on her way to the Hollywood Theatre, but probably never crossed the threshold. Her old-fashioned mother had a prejudice against apartments, and warned Beverly not to make friends with people who lived in them, because those people were not, as Mable put it, "substantial." Inside, hardwood floors, high ceilings, and archways are the sort of "substantial" details that most Portland residents now pay a premium for.

Next door to the apartments at Hancock and 41st is **SAM'S HOLLYWOOD BILLIARDS**, here since 1962.

Fred Meyer Hollywood, aka the Colossal Market ⑤
AT HANCOCK AND 41ST, TURN RIGHT. STOP FOR A MOMENT, MID-BLOCK.
Across 41st Avenue is a block-sized building. From 1931 to 1989, this was a Fred Meyer store, historic for its innovation, which was copied by other retailers across the country. (The building is now a Rite-Aid Pharmacy.)

Grocery shopping changed when Beverly was a young girl. For decades, Americans everywhere shopped for food and supplies at small corner grocery stores. In Portland a shop, often with the owners living upstairs, occupied just about every third corner, even

Rose City Park branch library where Beverly spent hours reading

in neighborhoods. Mothers would send their small children with a wagon to the grocer to pick up the daily phoned-in order. But in the 1920s, change had come. Safeway stores started appearing, and they were big: two storefronts wide. Then something bigger came along. In 1931, Portland grocer Fred G. Meyer, who had a downtown store, remodeled an auto service garage into a store here in the booming Hollywood District, right across from the theater. The "suburban" store, at first called the Hollywood Public Market, and its parking lot (a new idea) swallowed one entire block and was the first one-stop shopping store in the nation—a concept that was decades later adapted by Sam Walton, owner of Walmart, whom Meyer was friends with. The Hollywood store later expanded to fill the block, with parking on the roof.

Beverly called this market "The Colossal Market" in *Henry and Beezus*. The Fred Meyer store, with its sloping wooden floors that had you chasing your cart (and toddler in it), closed in 1989 when a newer one opened at Northeast Broadway and 30th Avenue.

That new Hollywood Fred Meyer is next to Sullivan's Gulch, where Beverly lived on Halsey Street when her family moved to Portland in 1922. That house is no longer there. Its lot was swallowed up by the Fred Meyer parking lot. (See the entry for 2843 NE Halsey Street in Chapter 4 for more on the history of the house and the gulch.)

Sandy Boulevard and the Hollywood Theatre 6

KEEP WALKING SOUTH ON 41ST AVENUE AND IN HALF A BLOCK COME TO SANDY BOULEVARD, one of Portland's oldest roads. Historically, it ran from the Sandy River at its confluence with the Columbia to the Stark Street Ferry. Today, segments have changed a bit, but it's essentially the same. Like many roads (such as Foster Road and Cully Boulevard) that predate the street grid system, it's a diagonal.

An East Portland history by the City of Portland notes the Sandy Road and other early roads followed ancient Native American paths. Oregon Trail pioneers used the path too: those who didn't

Farmers from outlying areas brought their produce into Portland on roads such as Sandy Boulevard, Scholls Ferry and Canyon Road. This farmer has a load of cauliflower.

walk the Barlow Trail over Mount Hood floated their goods down the Columbia River from The Dalles to the Sandy River. From the Sandy, they and their livestock walked the path into Portland. From Portland they kept on walking south to Oregon City, the seat of the provisional government before Oregon became a state. There, they filed their land claim.

A government survey of the Sandy Road was ordered in 1850, nine years before Oregon became a state. Later, farmers in the Columbia River bottomlands used the Sandy Road to bring their produce and wheat into Portland markets, crossing the Willamette via the ferry, and later via bridge.

Electric streetcars began running on Sandy Boulevard in 1907. It was only after a streetcar line went in that neighborhoods could be developed since most residents didn't own cars until the 1920s or later. These neighborhoods were considered Portland's first suburbs, though today they're described as "close-in."

Later, in the 1910s, as the State of Oregon began to improve its roads—most of which were still dirt or gravel—Sandy Boulevard became part of the developing Columbia River Highway, which ran from Astoria east to The Dalles and beyond.

Beverly knew this road well: she crossed it to get to the Hollywood Theatre at 41st and Sandy, and boarded the streetcar on it to ride downtown—or "overtown" as she called it, because you had to go over the river on a bridge to get there. She watched Queen Marie of Romania ride down Sandy Boulevard on a summer day in 1926. The Queen, a granddaughter of Britain's Queen Victoria, was a hero in World War I and a friend of Sam Hill, a Good Roads advocate and builder of the Maryhill Museum of Art. She came to Portland on a trip to dedicate Sam's new museum (although it did not officially open until 1940). Marie had toured the Columbia River Highway with Sam—another of his projects—and entered Portland by its then official "east entrance," Sandy Boulevard, and then proceeded into town via the Burnside Bridge, where she stayed at the Multnomah Hotel.

When you're standing at 41st and Sandy, in front of you is the fabulous **HOLLYWOOD THEATRE**. Opened in 1925, the Hollywood was the last Portland venue built as a combination vaudeville house and motion picture theater. John Bennes, better known for his elegantly simple Prairie-style homes, designed this peacock of a building. Look up at the terra cotta caryatids (columns shaped like women), mermaids, bearded warrior, ram's head, lyre-playing angel, putti (cherubic infants), and other colorful details that are more kin to Miami than grey-sky Portland. For ten cents, Beverly had her choice of its 1,500 seats.

The theater had an eight-piece orchestra that played during silent movies, which ran until 1927, when the first feature-length talking picture was released—*The Jazz Singer*. Today the Hollywood shows first run and independent movies, has live performances, and offers Hecklevision (where your snide texts show up onscreen), filmmaking courses, and more. The black marquee was new in 2013; it's based on the design of the original marquee. It replaced an awful midcentury white box that detracted from the building.

In *Otis Spofford*, Otis and his friends see a matinee here at the "Laurelwood." (Today a restaurant and brewery nearby are called the **LAURELWOOD**, a hybrid of Hollywood and nearby Laurelhurst.)

In *Henry and the Paper Route,* Henry's family heads to the Hollywood Theater to treat themselves after they all worked hard on a paper recycling drive that, due to Henry's entrepreneurial zeal, had been a little too successful. In that book, Beverly used the theater's true name.

FROM THE THEATER, TURN LEFT ON SANDY. At 43rd and Sandy is **PAULSEN'S PHARMACY.** Opened in 1918, it's the neighborhood's oldest business. In *Henry Huggins,* Henry walks home on Fridays "the long way" passing the Rose City Drugstore, the supermarket, and the barbershop and stopping at the pet shop where he would buy Ribsy two pounds of horsemeat. Go in and have ice cream at its soda fountain. Beverly remembered walking to the drugstore for Cokes with Claudine. In 2014, the store got a surprise 48-hour makeover. As part of that, antiques once stored in the basement are now on display.

Above the pharmacy was a wooden-floored dance studio. Students climbed a side stairway on 43rd Avenue to get to it. It is likely Beverly knew of this place: in *Ellen Tebbits,* the Spofford School of the Dance was upstairs above a Payless Drugstore. Ellen, about to

What a teenage Beverly saw as she walked to the Hollywood Theatre. The film on the marquee, *I am Suzanne*, was released in 1933. Small grocery stores like this one were on their way out, replaced by the larger Safeways and, in Hollywood, the new Fred Meyer store.

attend her first class, is tortured to think the other girls will realize she's wearing woolen underwear under her leotard. (In real life, Beverly was mortified by her mother's insistence that she wear long woolen underwear to school in winter.) Inside, Ellen meets her future best friend, Austine, whose own mother also forces her to wear long woolen underwear.

Beginning in 1984, the space was called the Children's Gym. Here, for decades, young parents climbed the side stairway and dropped kids off for tumbling classes. Today the space is District Collective, a photography studio with rental space for photo shoots and video production and the Children's Gym has moved further west on Sandy Boulevard.

Kitty-corner across Sandy at 43rd is the Beverly, an apartment building named for Beverly Cleary (what would her mother have thought of that?) with a **WHOLE FOODS** on the ground floor.

The old Hollywood Burger Bar, in an exuberant bit of early roadside architecture.

Along Sandy Boulevard through Hollywood each June is the Junior Rose Festival Parade, which any child can join in, wearing a homemade costume or riding a decorated bike. In *Henry and Beezus*, Beezus practices her baton twirling for the parade.

COME BACK TO THE INTERSECTION OF 42ND AND SANDY. In the northeast corner, for 60 years was the former Hollywood Burger Bar. Built in 1922, the Moorish design comes from its days as Allyn's Cleaner and Laundry. "As if by magic" was the slogan, complete with an Aladdin-like character on top.

Bikes, beer, and bathing suits on 42nd Avenue plus the Hollywood Library ⑦

FROM 42ND AND SANDY, WALK NORTH ON 42ND. There's nothing better than a locally run shop, and there are a couple of good ones in this stretch. First, if you like finding vintage bargains, visit **ANTIQUE ALLEY**

at the 42nd Street Station. The building started life in 1955 as one of eight Rodgers Stores, Portland variety stores that also sold home furnishings. The Rodgers lived upstairs in this mid-century modern building. Also inside are *AUNT TILLIE'S DELI, AND HIMALAYAN GIFTS AND CANDIES.*

Across the street is *VELO CULT BICYCLE SHOP AND TAVERN*, in a former antique mall. A bit further north is *POPINA SWIM AND SPORT*, locally designed and manufactured suits which make even middle aged bodies look good (ish). Next to it is the *MOON AND SIXPENCE* if you fancy a dark place to enjoy a cold pint.

FROM 42ND TURN LEFT ON TILLAMOOK STREET AND WALK ONE BLOCK TO THE HOLLYWOOD LIBRARY. Outside is *RUST COFFEE LOUNGE,* which serves coffee, vegan sweets, and other fare. Inside the library is a stone wall map honoring Beverly Cleary. The building was erected in 2002; upstairs are condominiums called the Bookmark. When Beverly was a child, this block was lined with Craftsman bungalows.

Klickitat Street and Beverly's home at 2924 NE 37th Avenue 8

The next stretch takes you through blocks of great old homes. *FROM THE LIBRARY'S FRONT DOOR, WALK NORTH ON 41ST AVENUE.* Immediately, you leave the commercial district. Homes here were initially built without garages. Notice how ingeniously garages were added over the years, often by carving out the front yard and digging out a basement space for the family's new Model T or Model A.

As you walk the long blocks northward, look for horse rings in the curbs. People in these neighborhoods never owned horses: they had access to one of the nation's most extensive streetcar systems,

When trucks began replacing horse-drawn wagons. This 1930 photo shows a load of cauliflower being delivered from a farm near Oswego Lake.

and, later cars of their own. But in the curbs you'll see iron horse rings, for tying up horses, straight out of the Old West. That's because when the curbs were poured, generally around 1910, many deliveries of ice, groceries or wood for heating were made via teams of horses. (Most Portland homes were heated in those years with wood or coal before converting to oil or gas.) Horse-drawn deliveries continued, though in dwindling numbers, through the 1930s. Find horse rings on your own, and if you want a hint, look at the curbs at 2205 and 2336 NE 41st.

Stop and ponder at two poetry posts, at 2221 and 2224 then **KEEP NORTH ON 41ST.** North of Brazee Street is a lineup of enormous elms that turn the sidewalk into a green or gold canyon, in season, in a block of gorgeous Craftsman and Foursquare-style homes.

STILL ON 41ST, CROSS KNOTT STREET. Eleven-year-old Henry Huggins has a paper route for the afternoon paper, the *Oregon Journal*. Every day, he picks up his batch of papers from Mr. Capper, the *Journal's* district manager, who lives on Knott Street in a home with a big horse chestnut tree.

Northeast 41st Avenue's elm tunnel in early autumn.

KEEP NORTH ON 41ST ONE MORE BLOCK TO ITS END AT STANTON. TURN LEFT ON THIS STREET, WHICH CURVES AS IT FOLLOWS THE BASE OF ALAMEDA RIDGE. ON STANTON, CROSS 40TH AND CÉSAR E. CHÁVEZ BOULEVARD (FORMERLY 39TH AVENUE), THEN TURN RIGHT ON 38TH. Here you get to climb the ridge, an 80 to 100-foot-high gravel hill left by Ice Age floods of 13,000 to 17,000 years ago. The rock that forms the ridge was carried here from as far away as the Rocky Mountains. As the floodwaters burst out of the Columbia River Gorge, swirling with ice chunks, trees, gravel, and soil, they hit Rocky Butte, churned around it, and slowed, dropping some of their load in this long, linear gravel deposit. From the Portland area, they roared down the Willamette Valley, flooding it as far south as Eugene, 100 miles away. Quite an event, and today the hill that the floods created has some of the best views and homes in town.

ON 38TH, CROSS WISTARIA DRIVE and notice how the neighborhood changes as developers a century ago tailored the homes' sizes and grandeur to the increasingly better views up the ridge. *IF YOU WANT TO CLIMB ONE OF ALAMEDA RIDGE'S 11 STAIRCASES, AN OPPORTUNITY PRESENTS ACROSS FROM 3041 NE 38TH. SEVENTY-EIGHT STEPS LIFT YOU TO THE TOP. TO STAY UP ON THE RIDGE FOR A BIT, TURN LEFT AT THE TOP OF THE STAIRS ONTO ALAMEDA STREET. FOLLOW IT AS IT CURVES LEFT, AND THEN GO LEFT ONTO KLICKITAT STREET. WALK TO 38TH AND KLICKITAT.*

IF YOU SKIPPED THE STEPS, KEEP WALKING NORTH ON 38TH, enjoying the narrow, peaceful street with homes that look like they jumped out of the pages of a storybook. It ends at Klickitat Street. Get out your phone for a selfie at the 38th Avenue and Klickitat Street sign.

When Beverly wrote her first book, she borrowed the characters from kids she knew on Hancock Street but changed the street name

One of Alameda Ridge's staircases, where you're likely to be greeted by a cat who may want some petting.

to Klickitat because she liked the knitting-needle sound of it. Henry, Beezus, and Ramona live on Klickitat Street.

The Klickitats are Native Americans whose homeland is on the east side of the Cascade Mountains, in Washington. Today they're part of the Confederated Tribes and Bands of the Yakama Nation. The Klickitat River and the community of Klickitat are named for them. The English botanist David Douglas first wrote the word in English in 1825, spelling it with a "C" instead of a "K." Some Native Americans spell it as *Klikitat*.

In June 1981, Beverly and Clarence Cleary rode at the head of a Children's Author Parade down Northeast Klickitat Street just west of here, between Irvington and Alameda schools. In a talk afterwards she said each book took her six months to a year to write, although she thought about them for three or four years before she actually began writing.

FROM KLICKITAT AND 38TH, WALK ONE BLOCK WEST ON KLICKITAT TO 37TH AND TURN LEFT TO WALK DOWNHILL for a couple of especially interesting blocks, if you like looking at beautiful homes. At Morris Street, you're off the ridge and into the land of more modest homes (if you can call today's $500,000-plus price tags modest). **NOT FAR PAST MORRIS IS BEVERLY'S HOUSE.**

The house at 2924 NE 37th was the home her parents bought after selling their Yamhill farm for $6,500 in 1927. The farm's buyer got 60 acres, an 1860 home (that still stands), Yamhill River frontage, fields and a wood lot. Factoring in inflation, that's $90,823 today, but that amount doesn't reflect how land values in the Willamette Valley soared as it became a world-renowned wine grape-growing region. Today, the valley is home to more than 400 wineries. The first commercial wineries in the valley started in the 1960s, forty years after the Bunns farmed there.

Beverly was in seventh grade at Fernwood when she moved to 37th, and her parents bought her a used bike to ride to school. After Home Ec class, the girls could take home the food they baked. She hung her food basket on her bike's handle bars, and would try to ride home as fast as she could before the boys would snatch the food off the bike and eat it. Riding on warped wooden rims, it was hard to get up enough speed to escape them.

Mable was especially proud of the home's two big plate glass windows. Sheltered by Alameda Ridge, the home is protected from the east winds that she had hated when they lived on 77th Street. (See the entry for 3600 NE 77th Ave. in Chapter 4.) But here, Lloyd's depression deepened. In Portland, with a series of indoor jobs, "his intelligence was wasted," Beverly wrote. He would often pull a wicker

Beverly's 37th Avenue home

chair out onto this porch. Hidden from neighbors by a curtain of Virginia creeper growing on a wire between porch columns, he would sadly whistle songs like "Bedelia" and "Smile Awhile." Years later, in *A Girl from Yamhill*, Beverly said that hearing those songs still filled her with grief.

Inside at night, Mable would read funny stories from the *Saturday Evening Post* aloud, to lift Lloyd's spirits. Her writing advice to the teenage Beverly was, "Try to write something funny. People enjoy reading anything that makes them laugh."

It wasn't all sad. In the driveway one night in 1932, 16-year-old Beverly waited for her date, a Reed College freshman, to open her car door and let her out. He refused: "Women can open their own doors these days," he said. She in turn refused to do it; they sat at an impasse. Then, worried what her mother would think of her sitting in a parked car with a boy, she rolled down the window and climbed out, her position, if not her dignity, intact.

The ceramic black and white house numbers on the house are originals, installed when Beverly was in high school. The house changed number from 632 to 2924 during Portland's great street renumbering, when the city's chaotic street names and numbers were finally wrangled into one sustainable system. See Chapter 2 for more on that.

The longtime owners of this home did not know when they bought it that it had been the home of Beverly Cleary. In a strange coincidence, one of them had gone to summer camp in California with Beverly and Clarence Cleary's twins, Malcolm and Maryanne.

In the room behind the large plate glass window, Mable coached Beverly in Latin, and Beverly entertained a suitor, Gerhart (a pseudonym) whom she detested but her mother loved, in a strange chapter in their relationship.

In *Henry Huggins*, Henry and his neighbor Scooter McCarthy stand on opposite sides of Klickitat Street and throw a football to

Beverly walked this 37th Avenue sidewalk to Grant High.

each other. Henry, however, loses the ball when a car passes just as he throws the ball and it sails through the car's open backseat window. The story, which truly happened here on 37th Avenue, was adapted by Beverly for her book, with one change. In real life, the ball was never returned.

Grant High and Grant Park 9

FROM BEVERLY'S HOUSE, KEEP SOUTH ON 37TH, on the same sidewalks she and best friend Claudine Klum walked to school for four years, past beautiful Portland homes which they would've known well. One spectacular exception is a home renovated in 2014 at 2721 NE 37th, in the Prairie style, with an enormous cantilevered overhang that defies gravity.

The school was originally built in 1925, soon after the Bunns moved into the neighborhood. Like most of Portland's public high schools, it's named for a U.S. president. General Ulysses S. Grant was stationed at nearby Fort Vancouver from 1852 to 1853 and was president from 1869 to 1877. In *Otis Spofford*, Beverly's poker-faced wit is seen in the name of the neighborhood high school: Zachary P. Taylor, who is often listed as one of the nation's worst or least memorable presidents. He died after just one year in office, in 1850.

Beverly found Grant to be less friendly than Fernwood, dominated as it was then by sororities and fraternities. In 1933, when she was a senior she co-wrote a play, *They Had to See Europe*, which was produced at school.

She kept good records of all her writing, and was able to recycle older works into chapters in her books. One story she wrote at Grant had to do with a practice we'd find reprehensible today. In the years before President Richard Nixon signed the Clean Water Act into law in 1972, it was common for factories to dump or pump their waste directly into rivers. That included everything from animal carcasses to chemicals. Beverly had read in the newspaper about a boy who had fallen into the river below a dye works and turned green from the dye that had been dumped there. She turned that news article into a short story at Grant called "the Green Christmas" and later into a chapter in *Henry Huggins*, where a can of green paint saves Henry from a dreaded role in a Christmas program.

FROM THE FRONT OF THE SCHOOL, WALK BACK NORTH ON 36TH TO THE PARK PATH THAT RUNS WEST FROM BRAZEE STREET. TURN LEFT INTO THE PARK AND WALK THE PATH THROUGH THE OFF LEASH DOG AREA. Leash laws didn't exist when Beverly lived here; they went into effect in 1960.

Beverly Cleary School, Hollyrood Campus, is on the right. Built in 1959 in the International style, it was part of a national wave of school building after WWII to accommodate the Baby Boomers. Just beyond the off leash area is a lawn with groves of towering Douglas firs. The rolling lawn is where Beverly once hunted night crawlers for fish bait when she was in college, "armed with flash lights and two quart jars." In *Henry Huggins*, Henry goes to Grant Park at dusk to catch night crawlers, which come out on the watered lawns. He'll earn one cent per worm from a neighbor who is going fishing on the Columbia.

Beverly remembered her first day of high school, walking up these steps on silken legs, in new stockings, on a day when distant forest fires had turned the sun into a "sullen orange ball," not unlike what still happens on late summer days in Portland.

As you walk west, look over at Grant High. Its enormous brick smokestack has been repurposed as a cell phone tower. Just below it to the west is the outdoor Grant High Pool, a noisy and popular place in summer.

In the park playground just before you get back to the sculptures, Henry and Beezus rub bread wrappers (which used to be made of waxed paper) on the metal slide to wax it, so they'll slide faster. The tall metal slide is gone, alas. Except for the danger-free modern play structure with its plastic slides, the taller trees, and the cell-phone smokestack, the park doesn't look that different than when Beverly Bunn played here with her friends.

FROM THE LAWN, WALK THE PARK PATHS TO RETURN TO THE START AT THE SCULPTURE GARDEN.

An Oregon Checklist: Beverly and Friends Were Here

2843 NE HALSEY STREET. Then called 869 Halsey Street, this was the first rental house the Bunns moved to when they left country life in Yamhill in 1922. It sits near the edge of Sullivan's Gulch, a natural depression created by the scouring action of Ice Age floods. The gulch originally was forested, with a creek running through it. Beginning in the 1850s, Timothy Sullivan farmed both sides of the gulch, from Broadway to Stark Street. Since 1883, the gulch has been the path of a rail line. When Beverly lived here, the land still showed remnants of its farm days, with cherry and plum trees and loganberry vines gone wild.

Beverly loved meeting city kids here, and played "brick factory" with the boys, pounding bricks they found into dust. She had first graders Ramona and Howie play this same game in *Ramona the Brave*.

The land later became industrialized but when Beverly lived here, it was still bucolic, with wild hazel bushes (filberts) growing on the gulch slopes, and a few trains each day passing by. She got smallpox while she lived here. The health department came over and nailed a red quarantine sign to the front of the house, warning people not to come near. She remembered one bright spot from her illness: her dad, who had moved out so as not to get sick, had Meier and Frank deliver cookies to his daughter.

The Halsey Street house had a wood and coal furnace. The Bunns would've ordered their fuel from Albina Fuel, just a few blocks away at Northeast 33rd and Broadway. The site today is a New Seasons Market and the Grant Park Place apartments.

In the 1930s, the gulch was home to a Hooverville, the name for shantytowns around the nation built by people left homeless by the Great Depression. Beginning in the 1950s the gulch became the route of a freeway, and in the 1980s, a light rail line. The Bunns' rental home is now gone. Today the site is part of the Fred Meyer Hollywood parking area. This is the second Fred Meyer in Portland's Hollywood neighborhood. See Walking with Ramona, Stop 5.

The Bunns lived in the Halsey Street house for only two years. Mable thought it was too close to the train tracks and the hobos who rode the rails in empty boxcars.

3600 NE 77TH AVE. The Bunns rented this home in 1924, when the house was two years old. Beverly was in third grade. Back then, its address was 770 77th Street N, five blocks from the city limits. Although streets had been platted out, houses were still widely spaced, with hazelnuts, currants and daisies growing wild. It was here that young Beverly, who had become a reluctant reader, fell in love with reading. On a rainy day she picked up a book that her mother had gotten at the library. She intended only to look at the pictures, but she suddenly found herself reading. She devoured the book and another one that same day. Her delighted mother even let her stay up late to finish the second one. The books were by Lucy Fitch Perkins about twins around the world having adventures.

In this house she wrote her first published work. The *Oregon Journal*, Portland's afternoon paper, offered books to students who would read and review them. She wrote a review of *The Story of Doctor Dolittle* by Hugh Lofting, and it was published in the paper.

Beverly rode sometimes to Gregory Heights School on the handlebars of a bike pedaled by an eighth-grader she had a crush on. He later helped the Bunns out by burying their dead cat, but made Beverly smolder by holding the dead cat by its tail. In *Beezus and*

Ramona, a dead family cat is treated with much more respect by the sisters.

The Bunns left the house after one icy winter in it, when they couldn't keep warm. Also, Lloyd didn't like the long streetcar ride to work as a floor man at West Coast National Bank (acquired by U.S. Bank in 1929).

3340 NE HANCOCK STREET. See the Walking with Ramona tour, Stop 3. After finding the 77th Street home to be too close to the icy gorge winds, the family chose this, their last rental home. Beverly lived here from fourth to seventh grade, 1925 to 1927.

2924 NE 37TH AVENUE. After selling their Yamhill farm in 1927, the Bunns had the cash to leave the renting life and buy this home, built in 1926. Formerly 632 E 37th St. N. See Walking with Ramona's Stop 8.

33RD AVENUE. In *Henry Huggins*, Henry wants to go sliding in his Flexible Flyer on the 33rd Street Hill. Northeast 33rd Avenue drops fast off Alameda Ridge from Fremont down to Knott Street. It's now too busy for sledding but wasn't when Beverly was a kid.

THE ARMORY. 128 NW 11th Ave. In March 1932 Beverly and 1,200 other girls attended the "Great Council Fire" for the city's Camp Fire Girls at the medieval-looking National Guard Armory. It was built in 1891 in anticipation of urban riots. Its vast interior without walls was designed so troops could practice maneuvers. Troops never had to train or march from it to combat a riot, so over the years, its wide-open space—the only covered large event space in town—was used when presidents came to Portland or for other events with large crowds. In 1932, at the Great Council Fire, Beverly's Camp Fire troop won a national honor for touring local factories, such as Jantzen

The Armory's vast stone-walled interior space is now divided into a coffee shop and theater.

Knitting Mills, and for corresponding with Camp Fire girls all over the world. They wrote one letter and copied it on a mimeograph machine—the ancestor to copying machines. Rival troops accused them of cheating, but they held their heads high and accepted the award. In 2006, the Armory's vast interior was re-envisioned and is now the Gerding Theater.

BANK OF CALIFORNIA. 330 SW Sixth Ave. After being hit with unemployment in 1930, Beverly's dad was relieved to be offered a job managing the safe deposit vault in the basement of this little terra cotta gem of a building, built in 1924.

BANKS, OREGON. Beverly's mom, Mable Atlee, moved from Michigan to the Pacific Northwest in 1905 to teach. Later, Mable's parents, W. S. and Mary Frances Atlee, left Michigan to join their daughter out West. They moved to tiny Banks, where they bought and operated the town's general store. In *In Search of Western Oregon,*

Ralph Friedman writes, "If you can get lost in Banks you should not be let out of the house." It was on the front porch of the store that Mable met her future husband, Lloyd Bunn. They were married in 1907. He was one of six brothers who grew up farming in Yamhill, Oregon. When Lloyd's father was gored by a bull and died a few years after he and Mable married, Lloyd took over the farm because none of his brothers wanted to.

BEAUMONT MIDDLE SCHOOL. 4043 NE Fremont St. In *Ramona Quimby, Age 8,* Beezus goes to Rosemont Junior High School, along with Otis Spofford and the girl he torments (because he likes her), Ellen Tebbits.

THE BEVERLY. 2025 NE 44th Ave. This apartment building at 44th and Sandy opened in 2009 and is named for Beverly Cleary, a fact that would likely have dismayed her mother. See the Walking with Ramona tour, Stop 4, for the reason.

BEVERLY CLEARY SCHOOL, FERNWOOD CAMPUS. 1915 NE 33rd Ave. See Walking with Ramona, Stop 2.

BEVERLY CLEARY SCHOOL, HOLLYROOD CAMPUS. 3560 NE Hollyrood Court. This International-style school on the north edge of Grant Park was built in 1958. It's in the small Hollyrood subdivision, platted in 1911 and now part of the Grant Park neighborhood. Students split their grade school years between this school and the Beverly Cleary School, Fernwood Campus (and at times, at Laurelhurst). See the Walking with Ramona tour at Stop 9 for more information.

BRIDAL VEIL, OREGON. When Beverly was in school for library science she interned one month in 1939 at the Portland Library Association (now Multnomah County Library). Spending time at various libraries, Beverly rode in the bookmobile that ran out to

Multnomah County towns to the east, including Bridal Veil in the Columbia River Gorge. It was a company town founded in 1886, with a sawmill (uphill in Palmer, Oregon) connected via flume to a planing mill in Bridal Veil. Both were shut down in 1936, about the time most of Larch Mountain's timber—the source for the mill—had been logged off. By the time of Beverly's visit, the mill in Bridal Veil was making wooden cheese boxes for Kraft Food Company. Cheese boxes were made in Bridal Veil until 1960. The mill closed for good in 1988 and was torn down in 2001, along with the company houses.

Today, except for the hiking trails, the busiest place in Bridal Veil is its post office. Engaged couples send wedding invitations from it, ensuring that even their postal stamp reinforces the wedding theme. Nearby is Bridal Veil Falls and the Bridal Veil Overlook, with spectacular gorge views. It's now a state park, and part of the Columbia River Gorge National Scenic Area.

CAMP NAMANU. Sandy, Oregon. In big trees on the Sandy River, this Camp Fire Girls camp opened in 1924 on 552 acres donated by lumberman Samuel B. Cobb. In *Ramona the Brave*, Ramona wears a hand-me-down tee shirt that says "Camp Namanu." In 1927, Beverly took a chartered camp train to Camp Namanu for two weeks while her stressed-out parents decided if they wanted to move back to the Yamhill farm. She didn't love being a camper, especially the cold swims in the Sandy River, but did like Namanu delight, a dessert of fruit mixed with whipped cream. When she returned to Portland, her parents had decided to sell the farm and stay in Portland.

CANYON ROAD. Today, Canyon Road starts as the Jefferson Street onramp to U.S. 26, and is then swallowed under the six lanes of that highway as it climbs to Sylvan Hill. From there it reappears and runs downhill into the Tualatin Valley, to Beaverton and beyond.

It's a historic market road, one that Tualatin Valley farmers used beginning in the 1840s to bring their vegetables, fruit and wheat into Portland. In the early 1930s, Beverly and her Camp Fire Girls troop rode out of Portland on this then two-lane road, which turned rural as soon as it entered

Portland's City Hall after a renovation restored its original beauty.

the West Hills. They would stop at a clearing along the road, build a fire, and then cook their food over it. The Sunset Highway beyond Sylvan Hill didn't exist.

CITY HALL. 1221 SW Fourth Ave. After Beverly got smallpox when she was in first grade, her house was put under quarantine. Before she was allowed to return to Fernwood Grammar School, her mother had to take her to the health inspector at City Hall, where she was certified to be safe.

DEE, OREGON. Beverly's friend Claudine Klum taught in this company town on the northern slopes of Mount Hood in the early 1930s, when the population was about 200. She boarded with a local family and was given the same lunch each day: white bread with sandwich spread and chopped pickles. Logging and fruit-growing were the industries. Some of Oregon's first Japanese immigrants settled in Dee. The town had a general store, shops, hotel and its own water works. In 1958, the town was dismantled by its new owner, Edward Hines Lumber Company. The dollars Claudine sent occasionally in her letters to Beverly, who was still a student at UC Berkeley, were much appreciated. Later in Claudine's life, Beverly bought her a Cadillac. Near Dee is the confluence of the East and West Forks of the Hood River, and the spectacular Punchbowl Falls, a beautiful hiking destination.

FEDERAL RESERVE BANK OF SAN FRANCISCO, PORTLAND. Corner of Southwest Fifth Avenue and Stark Street. The Federal Reserve system began in 1913, and the Portland bank opened in 1917 in the former Lumbermens National Bank with $6.5 million in gold reserves. When the Bunn family first moved to Portland in 1922, Beverly's dad got a job as a night guard at the Federal Reserve Bank. A replacement at 915 SW Stark St. was designed by 1949 by Pietro Belluschi.

FIRST CONGREGATION CHURCH. 1126 SW Park Ave. (now First Congregational Church of Christ). Beverly was a bridesmaid in April 1939 at her wealthy friend Virginia McCorkle's wedding to Robert Hayek. She wrote, in *My Own Two Feet*, how the expense involved was a hardship. The bridesmaids made their own dresses, giving them, Beverly wrote, a "loving hands at home" look that contrasted with the mother of the bride's elegant dress.

FRED MEYER HOLLYWOOD. 1814 NE 41st Ave. See the Walking with Ramona tour, Stop 5.

J.K. GILL'S. Southwest Fifth and Stark. Beverly appeared at this downtown bookstore in 1961 to sign books.

GOODWILL INDUSTRIES. Various Portland locations. One Halloween, Henry Huggins trick-or-treats at a neighbor's house. She doesn't have any candy but gives him a stuffed great horned owl that even Goodwill wouldn't take. Goodwill was started in 1902 in Boston as a Methodist church mission to collect used goods from wealthier sections of the city, repair them and redistribute them wherever they were needed. In 1915 it took its current name. Goodwill Industries of the Columbia Willamette is one of Goodwill Industries' 165 member organizations in the U.S. and Canada.

GRANT HIGH SCHOOL. 2245 NE 36th Ave. See Walking with Ramona, Stops 1 and 9.

GRANT PARK. Between Northeast 33rd and 36th avenues, north of U.S. Grant Place. See the start of the Walking with Ramona tour and its Stop 9.

HOLLYWOOD LIBRARY, NEW. 4040 NE Tillamook Street. See Walking with Ramona at Stop 7.

HOLLYWOOD LIBRARY, OLD. 3930 NE Hancock Street, now **FLEUR DE LIS** restaurant. See the Walking with Ramona tour's Stop 4.

HOLLYWOOD THEATRE. 4122 NE Sandy Blvd. See Walking with Ramona, Stop 6.

The Lotus Isle Amusement Park competed, from 1930 to 1933, with Jantzen Beach during Beverly's high school years. Here girls wait at the streetcar stop to the park. The Faloma Market in Northeast Portland and Lotus Isle City Park on Hayden Island are about all that remain.

IRVINGTON CLUB. 2131 NE Thompson St. In 1932, Beverly took lessons at this urban tennis and country club in Mrs. Kofeldt's ballroom dancing class. She was 16 then, and she writes in *A Girl from Yamhill* that her mother Mable said to her, "You're the sort who will fade quickly." It is here she met Gerhart (a pseudonym), a man six years older than she was, who began calling on her. His actions, described in *A Girl from Yamhill* and read with modern eyes, have the marks of a potential abuser. She tried repeatedly to rid herself of him, but her mother inexplicably kept encouraging Gerhart's attentions.

JANTZEN BEACH. On Hayden Island, in the Columbia River. Today it's the site of a shopping center, but for 40 years, it was an amusement park, swimming pool and ballroom. Streetcar companies often operated amusement parks at the end of their lines. (Oaks Park in Sellwood is the last remaining such park in Portland.) At Jantzen Beach, which opened in 1928 when she was twelve, Beverly danced as a teen when big bands performed in the ballroom. The park was a

project of Jantzen Knitting Mills; its giant swimming pools promoted swimming (and the purchase of Jantzen swimwear, of course).

JANTZEN KNITTING MILLS. 411 NE 19th Ave. and 1935 NE Glisan St. This Portland company revolutionized swimming in 1913 when it invented a lightweight knit that replaced heavy woolen swim suits. Its Art Deco-style factory building with the diving girl motif was designed in 1928. Swimsuits were made here from 1929 to 2002. Beverly toured the factory in 1932 when she was a Camp Fire Girl.

JOAN OF ARC STATUE. Northeast Cesar E. Chávez Blvd. and Glisan Street. This roundabout once was a streetcar stop and sales office for the Laurelhurst Company, where lots were sold for the Laurelhurst subdivision. After most of the lots had sold by the 1920s, the office was torn down and the circle became a park. Dr. Henry Waldo Coe donated the sculpture here and three others to the city. The others are Theodore Roosevelt and Abraham Lincoln (in the South Park Blocks downtown) and George Washington (at Northeast 57th Avenue and Sandy Boulevard). Coe started the Morningside Hospital, a psychiatric facility at Southeast Stark and 96th Avenue that operated from 1910 to 1968. Beverly remembered, in *A Girl from Yamhill*, "We saw the statue of Joan of Arc unveiled and were bored by the speeches."

JUNIOR ROSE FESTIVAL PARADE. Along Sandy Boulevard, every June, as part of Portland's Rose Festival. In *Henry and Beezus*, Beezus practices twirling her baton to walk in the parade. Any kid can be in it. And when Ramona makes a crown for herself out of burdock burs, her dad asks if she thinks she's a Rose Festival Queen.

KLICKITAT STREET SIGN AT 37TH AVENUE. See Walking with Ramona, Stop 8.

KNOTT STREET. See the Walking with Ramona tour, Stop 8.

LAFAYETTE, OREGON. Beverly named her doll Fordson-Lafayette. Fordson for her Yamhill neighbor's tractor, and Lafayette for the Willamette Valley town her great grandfather Hawn had settled in, near Yamhill. Ramona is also prone to naming her dolls after corporate products: Bendix (a washing machine) and Chevrolet (a car).

LAURELHURST PARK. Between Southeast 33rd Ave. and Cesar E. Chávez Blvd., and Ankeny and Stark streets. In *Otis Spofford*, Ellen Tebbits gets her revenge on Otis, who had cut her braids off during a classroom melee. While he's skating on the frozen lake in Laurelwood Park, she and best friend Austine carry his boots and shoes away, leaving him to hobble and wobble on his skates to the bus and then home. The real lake in the park is called Firwood Lake, and it's an expanded cattle watering hole. The land had been owned by W. S. Ladd, one of Portland's early entrepreneurs, who had a hobby farm here and ran cattle on the land.

LAURELHURST SCHOOL. 840 NE 41st Ave. In *Ramona Quimby, Age 8*, Ramona has to ride the bus to a new school, Cedarhurst Primary School, because her old school, Glenwood, had become an intermediate school. Cedarhurst, like Laurelhurst, is a two-story red-brick building. Her second floor classroom looked out over the trees to Mount Hood, just as Beverly's eighth-grade classroom did at Fernwood.

LONDON PLAZA APARTMENTS. 4010 NE Hancock Street. It was built in 1926, when Beverly Bunn was 10. See Walking with Ramona, Stop 4.

McMINNVILLE, OREGON. Willamette Valley. When she was nine months pregnant in 1916, Beverly's mom, Mable Bunn, took the train from Yamhill to McMinnville, 17 miles away, and checked into the hospital. Her plan was to stay until her baby was born. In the week she waited, she helped the nurses mop the floors and handle other housekeeping chores. The hospital was at Adams and Baker streets, about where a Walgreens now sits.

MEIER AND FRANK BUILDING. 621 SW Fifth Ave. After a visit to

her orthodontist nearby in the Selling Building, Beverly would wander the aisles of Meier and Frank department store and visit the Central Library before taking the streetcar back to Northeast Portland.

MENUCHA. Corbett, Oregon. While Beverly

was in school for library science, the library bookmobile took her near Crown Point at Menucha, the summer home of the family of Governor Julius Meier. Governor Meier had died in 1937, and his family sold the estate to the Presbyterian Church in 1950. Today Menucha is a retreat and conference center.

MILLS OPEN AIR SCHOOL. 511 SE 60th Ave. Beverly Bunn's dreaded first grade teacher, Miss Falb, was transferred to this school for children with tuberculosis. In the days before antibiotics, it was thought that the air on hills, such as here on Mount Tabor's slopes, would help cure TB patients. Windows were kept open during the winter and children often took naps on the lawn outside. Today the building is a YMCA child development center.

MULTNOMAH COUNTY LIBRARY, CENTRAL LIBRARY. 801 SW 10th Ave. Beverly remembers her mother taking her to the Portland Library Association, as it was called in the 1920s, with its marble floors. Central Library opened in 1913. Beverly also visited this library on her many solo trips downtown during her six-year-long orthodontia odyssey. In 1990 the Library Association transferred its assets to Multnomah County.

MULTNOMAH FALLS. In the Columbia River Gorge National Scenic Area. Beverly's ancestors came to Oregon in 1843, in the first big wagon train. They bought canoes from Indians in The Dalles to ride the Columbia River down the last leg of the journey. It was winter, and just opposite Multnomah Falls, the party was blown ashore by strong east winds. Beverly and her parents took drives out the Columbia River Highway in their Model A Chevrolet 80 years later. Beverly and her dad climbed into the cave behind the falls, a practice no longer allowed, at this, Oregon's most visited tourist attraction, where you'll hear more languages spoken than at any other place in the state.

MULTNOMAH STADIUM (NOW PROVIDENCE PARK). 1844 SW Morrison St. In *Ribsy*, Ribsy jumps out of the car window when the family is shopping, then escapes from his rescuers, who've taken him to the west side of Portland. On his trek back home, he thinks he's found his boy Henry Huggins when he sees kids from Zachary Taylor High cheering "outside a concrete stadium" where their team is playing Chester A. Arthur High. Ribsy disrupts the game then goes home with a boy who lives in one of the apartment buildings around Northwest 20th and Burnside near the stadium. In real life, when they were Grant High students, Beverly and her friend Claudine rode a chartered streetcar to watch Grant play football games here.

OREGON CITY, OREGON. In 1843, Beverly's ancestor Jacob Hawn was hired to build a mill here, at Willamette Falls by the Hudson's Bay Company. The falls are the largest in the Pacific Northwest, by volume, and for millennia a major Native American fishing and trading site.

OREGON HUMANE SOCIETY. 1067 NE Columbia Blvd. In *Ribsy*, Ribsy jumps out of the Huggins's car window while they're shopping. He gets lost, and is picked up by people who drive the wrong way— not back to Portland's east side where he lives, but across the river (the Willamette), past tall buildings (downtown), up a canyon (the Jefferson Street onramp to today's U.S. 26) and out of the city to a subdivision of new homes off the highway (Cedar Mill or West Slope, for example). See Multnomah Stadium entry. Henry's dad, after Ribsy's been gone a while, says they can get another dog at the Humane Society.

The Oregon Humane Society is the nation's third oldest. It was founded in 1868 to end the abuse and neglect of draft animals—horses and oxen. Until 1933 its mission included protecting orphaned children. In 1918, it moved into a 4-acre farm in Northeast Portland. Today it's still there; at its very busy shelter, more than 11,000 animals walk or get carried out the door each year to their new homes.

PAULSEN'S PHARMACY. 4246 NE Sandy Blvd. See Walking with Ramona, Stop 6 and the listing in Chapter 5 for this, one of the last places in Oregon where you can order a float at a drugstore soda fountain.

PORTLAND STATE UNIVERSITY. 1825 SW Broadway. In 1979's *Ramona and her Mother,* Mr. Quimby goes back to school at Portland State to become an art teacher. The school didn't exist when Beverly lived in Portland. It began in 1946 in a converted shopping mall as the Vanport Extension Center, named for its location in the wartime town of Vanport, which disappeared in a flood one day in May 1948.

PORTLAND VAN AND STORAGE. 407 N Broadway. This ornate building with its clinker brick and Gothic-style arches went up in 1925 during one of Portland's real estate booms. Beverly would've passed this as she traveled from Northeast Portland into downtown over the Broadway Bridge. In *Ramona and her Father,* Mr. Quimby works at a van and storage place, but loses his job after a bigger company buys out his employer. Mrs. Quimby worries about their property taxes, which are due in November, just as they continue to be every November in Portland.

PUDDING RIVER. Near Canby, Oregon. Beverly went many times to Claudine Klum's family cabin on the Pudding, on land owned by the Colvin family. Their Pudding River Campground and Picnic

Resort was a popular weekend getaway for Portlanders in the early 1930s. The Pudding, or "Puddin'" as Beverly and Claudine called it, flows into the Molalla River in Molalla River State Park in Canby.

Its unusual name came about around 1812. French-Canadian fur trappers Joseph Gervais and Etienne Lucier camped along it and shot an elk. Blood pudding, a French dish, was made and enjoyed by all. The men gave the river the name *Riviere au Boudin*, or Pudding River.

QFC. 1835 NE 33rd Ave. The site of Abendroth's Market and the grocery where Ramona lost her boot. See the Walking with Ramona tour, Stop 1.

RAMONA APARTMENTS. 1550 NW 14th Ave. Appropriately located on Quimby Street in the Pearl District, this building is geared to

Where Beverly learned to read fast, by reading silent movie titles

families. A Portland Public School kindergarten operates here called Chapman at the Ramona.

REED COLLEGE. 3203 SE Woodstock Blvd. As a high school junior Beverly went to some dances at Reed College Commons with a Reed boy.

ROCKAWAY, OREGON. The summer of 1927 Beverly became very ill. A doctor said she was malnourished and needed to run on the beach. So the family packed up a trunk of cooking utensils and clothes and took the train from Portland to Rockaway Beach, where for two weeks they stayed in a one-room cottage, swam in the ocean every day and raked crabs from tide pools. In July 1927, the *Oregonian* ran an article reporting the throngs of city dwellers who visited the beach that month and included this line: "Mr. and Mrs. C.L. Bunn and Miss Beverly Bunn of Portland are visiting the beach for two weeks and are staying in one of the cottages in Gray's Driftwood camp."

Ross Hollywood Chapel, before its green paint scheme

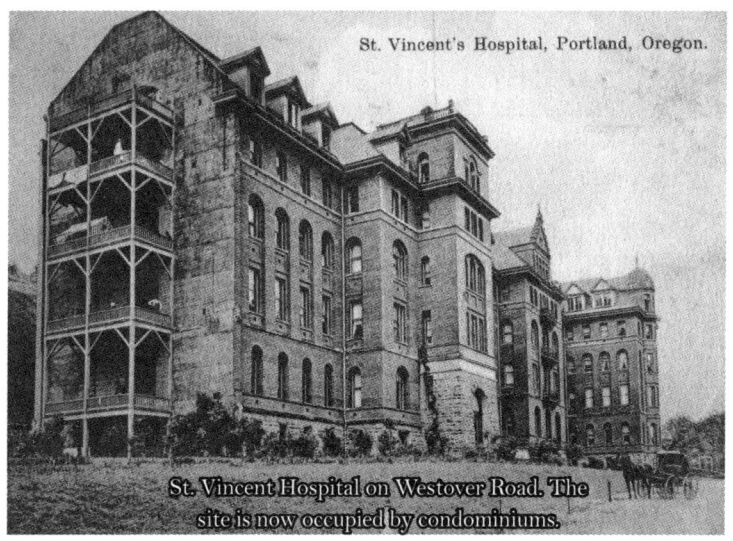

St. Vincent Hospital on Westover Road. The site is now occupied by condominiums.

ROSE CITY PARK PRESBYTERIAN CHURCH. 1907 NE 45th Ave. Beverly was raised a Presbyterian and attended Sunday School. She does not name which church she went to, but this one, which began in 1909, with the sanctuary constructed in 1925, is a likely candidate, as she notes she would walk to Sunday School.

ROSEWAY HEIGHTS SCHOOL (FORMERLY GREGORY HEIGHTS GRAMMAR SCHOOL). 7334 NE Siskiyou St. In the one year—her third grade year—that Beverly and her parents lived on 77th Street, she attended Gregory Heights. The school building was new in 1923.

ROSEWAY THEATER. 7229 NE Sandy Blvd. Her third grade year, when Beverly lived on 77th Street, she went to see silent movies at this new theater. After she learned to read in second grade she refused to read books outside of school, but she did learn to read fast here, by reading the title cards at the bottom of the screen. She mentions *The*

Sea Hawk (1924) as a great pirate movie. The theater was renovated in 2008.

ROSS HOLLYWOOD CHAPEL. Beverly's dad, Chester Lloyd Bunn, was buried at Pike Cemetery in Yamhill in October 1951. He died in Portland at age 64. His funeral service was held here, in this mid-century neighborhood landmark.

ST. JOHNS LANDFILL. Off North Columbia Boulevard. This landfill—a former wetland—saw its last load of garbage delivered in 1991. Now Portland's garbage gets trucked to Arlington, in eastern Oregon, and the landfill has been covered with soil and renamed St. Johns Prairie. In *Henry and the Clubhouse*, Henry gets a ride in an

old clawfoot bathtub tied to a trailer. His neighbor, Mr. Grumbie, who is modernizing his bathroom, is hauling it down Lombard Street toward the dump.

ST. VINCENT'S HOSPITAL. Formerly on Northwest Westover Terrace in the Nob Hill neighborhood. Beverly had her tonsils removed here when she was in sixth grade. The Catholic hospital, a huge stone castle of a building, was erected in 1892. It was torn down in 1979 and replaced by the current Providence St. Vincent Medical Center on Southwest Barnes Road.

SANDY BOULEVARD. See the Walking with Ramona tour, Stop 6 for info on this historic road.

SELLING BUILDING. 610 SW Alder St. When Beverly's parents sold their Yamhill farm in 1927, they had enough money to have Beverly's teeth fixed. For six years she went to Dr. P. T. Meaney, an orthodontist in the Selling Building. His office was at 902. The building had been completed in 1910. Despite Dr. Meaney's name, Beverly writes that he was a kind man. The building is named after another kind man, Ben Selling, a Portland businessman, philanthropist and humanitarian. He defended Chinese residents in the 1880s when some Portlanders tried to exclude them from the city, and he organized local resettlement efforts for thousands of Jewish refugees who fled persecution in Eastern Europe beginning in the 1890s.

SWAN ISLAND. In the Willamette River just north of downtown Portland. Beverly used to drive with Gerhart out to Swan Island in the early 1930s to watch the nightly mail plane land at the Swan Island Airport, an exceptionally lovely urban airport with runways lined with cherry trees. In 1927 she had seen Charles Lindbergh, the famous aviator, parade through town, after he'd become the first

One of the last original cherry trees on Swan Island

person to fly solo across the Atlantic Ocean. Lindberg had visited the then-new Swan Island Airport and pronounced it a terrible place to put an airport. By the 1930s, crews were filling in the Columbia Slough to prepare the land for a new airport, today's PDX. In WWII, Swan Island became home to a Kaiser shipyard that made wartime ships. Today it's an industrial park. A few cherry trees remain.

TILLAMOOK STREET. See the Walking with Ramona tour, Stop 1.

UMPQUA RIVER. Southwest Oregon. In *Henry and Ribsy*, Henry's friend Scooter McCarthy has gone fishing on the Umptucca River—a blend of Oregon's Umpqua and Nestucca rivers, two rivers that flow from the Coast Range into the Pacific Ocean.

YAMHILL, OREGON. Willamette Valley. The Bunn family's Yamhill home was built in 1860, and purchased in the 1870s by Beverly's grandparents John Marion Bunn and Mary Edith Amine Hawn

Beverly's home in Yamhill

Bunn. Her father Lloyd grew up in it, and after he married, lived in it with his wife Mable, and young daughter Beverly. In *A Girl from Yamhill*, Beverly writes that her first memory is of all the church bells in Yamhill ringing at once, celebrating the end of World War I. At family gatherings, Beverly, still a preschooler herself, had to be nice to her younger cousin Barbara, a duo recreated in the Ramona series, in Ramona's relationship with Willa Jean, the obstreperous younger sister of her friend Howie.

In *Beezus and Ramona*, Ramona is caught one day in the basement, taking one delicious bite out of every apple in a bushel and then discarding it. This story came right out of Beverly's Yamhill days: she used to sit under the apple tree, taking one bite each out of windfall apples because, of course, the first bite tastes the best. Her mother didn't care: there were plenty of apples to go around. She grew up there free to ramble the 80 acres and explore and play without much supervision, trusted to follow the rules her parents had laid out. Her mother taught her, "Never be afraid."

YMCA, DOWNTOWN. In *Henry Huggins*, Henry takes the bus on Wednesdays to swim at the "downtown YMCA." The old YMCA was built in 1909 at Southwest Sixth and Yamhill and Taylor. It was central to the Portland Vice Scandal of 1912–1913 in which Portland's gay subculture was exposed. That was an era when homosexuality was against the law. The building was razed in the 1970s. See also the next entry.

YMCA, HOLLYWOOD (NOW THE NORTHEAST COMMUNITY CENTER). 1630 NE 38th Ave. Formerly the Northeast Portland YMCA, this elegant building went up in 1925, the same year as Grant High and the Hollywood Theatre. Its three-lane, 20-meter indoor pool is where Scooter McCarthy goes to swim in *Henry and the Paper Route*. Scooter asks Henry Huggins to fold his papers for him so he can swim a little longer before he has to deliver them. This opens a career pathway for Henry, who has longed for a route of his own. In 2004, the YMCA announced plans to close the facility. The community rallied and purchased the building and continue its programs.

5

*Eat, Drink, and Shop
in Hollywood*

Eat and Drink

*On or very near the Walking with Ramona tour route

AUNT TILLIE'S DELI AND PUB * Since 1984, good sandwiches and soups, in the 42nd Street Station. Monday to Friday, 9:30 am to 7 pm; Saturday to 5 pm 2000 NE 42nd Ave. 503-281-1834

BASKIN ROBBINS * Ice cream, A half-block off the tour route. 1815 NE César E. Chávez Blvd. 503-284-6478 Mon–Sun 11:00 AM–10:00 PM.

BLIND ONION PIZZA AND PUB Get the General's pizza, named for the Grant Generals, the high school team nearby. Daily 11 am to 10 pm 3345 NE Broadway. 503-284-2825

THE BULGOGI * Korean food. 4232 NE Sandy Blvd. 503-327-8607 Monday to Friday 11:30 am to 8:30 pm (closed 3 to 4:30 pm) Sat 11:30 am - 8:00 pm, Sun 12:00 pm - 7:00 pm

COLUMBIA RIVER BREWING COMPANY * Brew pub fare. Daily 11 am to 10 pm/ to 11 pm Friday and Saturday. 1728 NE 40th Ave. 503-943-6157.

FLEUR DE LIS BAKERY AND CAFÉ * French pastries, local foods and coffee from the former manager of the Hollywood Farmers Market, in the atomic-era former Hollywood Library building. Monday to Friday 7 am to 4 pm; Saturday and Sunday 8 am to 3 pm Live music on Saturdays. 3930 NE Hancock St. 503-459-4887 Live music on Saturdays, from 10AM-12:30PM

FRED MEYER HOLLYWOOD In the far reaches of its parking lot, six-year-old Beverly lived in a house at Northeast 28th and Halsey (now gone). Before Fred Meyer moved in in 1989, some of the homes had been torn down and the site industrialized as the Pacific Steel Warehouse

Company. Nearby homes from the early 1900s, on Weidler Street remain from its once residential past. Daily 7 am to 11 pm 3030 NE Weidler St. 503-280-1300

HOLLYWOOD FARMERS MARKET April to Thanksgiving: every Saturday morning; December to March: first and third Saturday mornings. Northeast Hancock St between 44th and 45th avenues. November-April: 1st and 3rd Saturdays. Saturday 8-1pm. Rest of the year, weekly. Hours subject to change. Sister Market (close by): Every Saturday 10am – 2pm Oregon Square Courtyard, 800 NE Holladay St.

HOTLIPS PIZZA One in a chain of six Portland-based pizza and local soda shops. In the Pal's Shanty Tavern building, which from 1937 to 2014 occupied this former silent-movie theater. Daily 11 am - 10 pm 4630 NE Sandy Blvd. 503-284-4046

KILLER BURGER One in a chain of seven gourmet burger restaurants. Beer too. Daily 11 am to 10 pm (to 8 pm Sunday). 4644 NE Sandy Blvd. 971-544-7521

LAUGHING PLANET * Newest in a Portland-based chain of vegetarian burritos and bowls. Daily 11 am to 9 pm 1914 NE 42nd Ave. 503-281-2326

LAURELWOOD PUBLIC HOUSE AND BREWERY Flagship location, with rooftop deck. Try the award-winning Workhorse IPA. 5115 NE Sandy Blvd. Daily from 11am to 10pm. 503-282-0622

THE MAGNOLIA: A BEER AND WINE BAR * With small plates and sandwiches. Tuesday to Thursday 4 to 11 pm; Friday and Saturday 4 pm to 12 am. Happy Hour, Every Day 4pm-6pm & 10pm-Close. Minors ok before 7pm. Restaurant is vegetarian and vegan friendly. 4075 NE Sandy Blvd. 503-459-4081

Pal's Shanty Tavern, at Northeast 46th and Sandy. It occupied an old silent movie theater for years. It's now a Hotlips Pizza.

MOON AND SIXPENCE · British pub fare with good beer selection. Daily 3 pm to 2:30 am Kids okay 3 to 9 pm 2014 NE 42nd Avenue. 503-288-7802

MY CANH · Vietnamese and Chinese food. Daily except Sunday: 11 am to 9 pm 1801 NE Cesar E. Chávez Blvd. 503-281-0594.

NECTAR CAFÉ · Vegan and vegetarian food, juices and coffee. Daily 7:30 am to 8 pm / Weekends from 8 am 1925 NE 42nd Ave., Suite D (west of 42nd in a strip mall near the U.S. Bank). 971-302-6359

New Seasons Market Portland-based organic and local grocery and deli (with non-organic choices too). At Grant Park Village, 213 apartments built at the former site of Albina Fuel. Monday to Friday. Daily 8 am to 10 pm 3210 NE Broadway. 503-282-2080

Nicholas Restaurant A refugee from Lebanon, Nicholas Dibe, started a restaurant in 1985 on Southeast Grand Avenue. This is one of two other outposts of fantastic Lebanese and Mediterranean fare. Weekdays 11am to 8pm, Weeknights till 9pm, (opens at noon on Sunday). 3223 NE Broadway. 503-445-4700

Paulsen's Pharmacy · One of the last drugstore soda fountains in Oregon. Here since 1918. Weekdays 9 am to 6 pm. Saturday 9am to 5:00pm, closed Sunday. 4246 NE Sandy Blvd. 503-287-1163

QFC · Chain grocery store across from Fernwood School, at the location of Abendroth's Grocery, which awarded a young Beverly Cleary a $2 prize for winning a writing contest. Open 24/7. 1835 NE 33rd Avenue. 503-284-9901

Rust Coffee Lounge · At the front door of the current Hollywood Library. Food, beer and wine too. Monday to Friday 6 am to 6 pm; Saturday and Sunday 7 am to 6 pm 2035 NE 41st Ave. 503-282-2589

Sam's Hollywood Billiards · Take a break from your walking tour with a game of pool and a burger. Monday-Thursday, Sunday: 7:00 am-12:30 am. Friday, Saturday: 7:00 am-1:30 am. 1845 NE 41st Ave. 503-282-8266

Shandong Restaurant Northern Chinese cuisine. Daily 11 am to 9:30 pm (closed 2:30 to 4 pm). Happy hour meal prices 4 to 6 pm 3724 NE Broadway. 503-287-0331

Paulsen's Pharmacy, before its 2014 renovation

SUSHI CHIYO One of two local Portland-Vancouver based bars. Daily 11 am to 10 pm Plates $1.85 each from 2 to 4:30 pm Happy Hour: 4pm-6pm. 4029 NE Sandy Blvd. 503-288-4858

VELO CULT BIKE SHOP AND TAVERN · Bikes, beer, coffee, and deli sandwiches. Tuesday to Saturday 10 am to 10 pm; Sunday and Monday 11 am to 7 pm 1969 NE 42nd St. 503-922-2012

VIVIENNE KITCHEN AND PANTRY · Breakfast and lunch, cocktails too; next to the theater. 9 am to 2 pm Tuesday to Sunday. 4128 NE Sandy Blvd. 5 to 9 pm, Friday and Saturday. Saturday, 9:00 am - 2:00 pm, 5:00 pm - 9:00 pm. 503-384-2473.

WHOLE FOODS MARKET* On the ground floor of the Beverly Apartments, named to honor Beverly Cleary. Daily 7 am to 10 pm 4301 NE Sandy Blvd. 503-284-2644

Shop

*On or very near the Walking with Ramona tour route

ANTIQUE ALLEY* 100 dealers in the basement at 42nd Street Station. 2000 NE 42nd Ave. 503-287-9848 Monday through Friday: 10am-6pm, Saturday 10am-5:30pm, Sunday 12-5pm

BROADWAY CIGAR In a WWII Quonset hut. For the aficionado or the curious. Monday to Saturday 10 am to 9 pm; Sunday 11 am to 6 pm 3615 NE Broadway. 503-473-8000

GOLDEN TREASURES GIFT SHOP* Handcrafted toys, clothes, baby goods, and kitchenware. Weekdays 9:30 am to 4 pm 1820 NE 40th Ave. 503-288-8303

HIMALAYAN GIFTS AND CANDIES* Monday to Friday 10:30 am to 6 pm; Saturday to 5:30 pm In the 42nd Street Station. 2000 NE 42nd Ave. 503-284-8409

THE HOBBY SMITH* A half-block off the tour route. Where to get your model train fix; afterwards grab a cone from Baskin Robbins next door. 1809 NE César E. Chávez Blvd. (renamed 39th Avenue). Monday-Friday: 10:00 am - 6:00 pm, Sat: 10:00 am - 5:00 pm, Sun: 12:00 pm - 4:00 pm, 503-284-1912

JUST 4 KIDS • Longtime retail shop. 1925 NE 42nd Ave., Suite F. 503-249-7556 Monday-Friday, 9:30 am - 5:00 pm. Saturday, 10:00 am - 4:00 pm, Sunday: Closed.

LITTLE AXE RECORDS • Vinyl and cassettes from around the planet. Noon to 7:30 pm daily. 4142 NE Sandy Blvd. 503-816-9081

MOUNTAIN SHOP Local store, founded in 1937 (formerly at Northeast Seventh and Broadway). Now in the former Steigerwald Dairy building. Weekdays 10 am to 7 pm; Saturday 10 am to 6 pm; Sunday 12 to 5 pm 1510 NE 37th Ave. 503-288-6768

POPINA SWIM AND SPORT • Inspired by the look of the 1940s and 50s. A Portland-based, woman-owned firm that sells nationwide and in Canada. One of two Portland shops. Monday-Wednesday: 10am-6pm, Thurs-Sat: 10am-7pm, Sunday: 12pm-5pm 2030 NE 42nd Ave. 503-282-5159

PORTLAND PASTIMES • Toys, games, puzzles, magic. Weekdays 10am-6pm, Sat: 9am-6pm, Sun: 10am-5pm 1925 NE 42nd Ave., Suite B. 503-327-8353

RAY'S RAGTIME • Vintage clothes and treasures. 4059 NE Sandy Blvd. Mon-Fri 11-6pm, Sat 12-6pm, Sun 1-6pm.

RITE-AID PHARMACY • The usual thing, but in a historic building: where Fred Meyer created his first "suburban" one-stop shopping store in 1931 (and updated in 1950), a concept later adapted by Walmart. The Freddies closed in 1989 and the Hollywood store moved to its current location. Daily 7 am to 10 pm 1814 NE 41st Ave. 503-249-7627

SPARK ARTS CENTER • A half-block off the tour route. Art and craft supplies, plus classes. Weekdays 9 am to 6 pm Saturday 10 am to 5 pm Sunday 12 to 4 pm 1805 NE César E. Chávez Blvd. (the renamed 39th Avenue). 503-281-6757

TEAL FLAMINGO˙ Vintage clothes and hair salon. 1925 NE 42nd Ave., Suite D 971-279-2262, Closed Monday & Sunday, Tues-Fri 11-7pm, Sat, 10-6pm

A

Appendix:
Portland-based Books
by Beverly Cleary

Portland-Based Books

1950	*Henry Huggins*	
1951	*Ellen Tebbits*	
1952	*Henry and Beezus*	
1953	*Otis Spofford*	
1954	*Henry and Ribsy*	
1955	*Beezus and Ramona*	
1957	*Henry and the Paper Route*	
1962	*Henry and the Clubhouse*	
1964	*Ribsy*	
1968	*Ramona the Pest*	
1975	*Ramona the Brave*	
1977	*Ramona and her Father*	Newberry Honor Book
1979	*Ramona and her Mother*	National Book Award
1981	*Ramona Quimby, Age 8*	Newberry Honor Book
1984	*Ramona Forever*	
1999	*Ramona's World*	

Also Set in Oregon

Autobiographies

B

Appendix:
Getting to the Tour by
Bus, Bike, Foot, or MAX
+ Where To Rent Bikes

T he Walking with Ramona tour begins at the west side of Grant Park, at Northeast 33rd Avenue and Brazee Street.

BUS-WALK COMBO

From downtown Portland, the quickest bus is the Number 12, which runs every 15 to 20 minutes daily. Ride it from Southwest Sixth Avenue and Yamhill Street and get off at Northeast Sandy Boulevard and 33rd Avenue. Walk 0.75 mile to the start of the walking tour: From the bus stop, cross Sandy Boulevard and walk left (north) on 33rd, crossing I-84 and busy Northeast Broadway. It's not a super pleasant walking experience until you get nearer Grant Park.

From the Lloyd District, the quickest route is to board the Number 70 bus at Northeast 11th Avenue and Holladay Street. It runs every 15 to 20 minutes daily. Ride it approximately 10 minutes and request the stop at Northeast 33rd Avenue and Brazee Street, the starting point for the Walking with Ramona tour.

TRAIN-BUS-WALK COMBO

You can also ride the Blue Line MAX train, boarding at various stations downtown and in the Lloyd District. Get off at the first station east of the Lloyd District, the Hollywood/Northeast 42nd Avenue Transit Center. From the train tracks, take the elevator or stairs to the pedestrian overpass and turn left, which leads to the bus area of the transit center.

There, catch the Number 75 bus, which runs every 15 to 20 minutes daily. Ride it 0.6 mile north, requesting a stop at Northeast 42nd Avenue and Brazee Street. From there, walk west on Brazee. When it ends at Grant Park, continue west through the park on a path to the start of the tour. It's a 0.5-mile walk from the bus stop to the start of the tour.

TRAIN-WALK COMBO

Or instead of taking the Number 75 bus from the MAX stop, just start walking from the Hollywood Transit Center. It's 1.1 miles from the MAX stop to the start of the Walking with Ramona tour. Except for a stretch along Northeast 42nd Street, this route won't duplicate the streets you'll be exploring on the tour: From the MAX stop, take the elevator or stairs to the pedestrian overpass and turn left to come off the overpass and down to Halsey Street. From there, go north on Northeast 42nd Avenue. At Broadway, jog right to stay on 42nd. Cross Sandy Boulevard and now you're in the commercial heart of Hollywood. From 42nd, turn west on Tillamook, and pass the Hollywood Library, which offers a restroom break. Continue west on Tillamook, which changes names at 37th Avenue to U.S. Grant Place. At 33rd, turn right and walk two blocks to the start, 33rd and Brazee.

TRIMET TICKET INFO

TriMet operates the Portland area's public transit system. Trimet. org or 503-238-RIDE. Its Trip Planner gives you bus, train, bike and walk options from wherever you are. One ticket is good for the bus, streetcar and MAX light rail trains. Tickets cost $1.25 or $2.50 depending on your age and are good for a return trip if it's within two and half hours. An all day ticket is $2.50 or $5.

RENT BIKES

PEDAL BIKE TOURS: ebikes-city bikes-road bikes. Downtown near a MAX light rail stop. Bike to Hollywood/Grant Park (about 4 miles via quieter side streets) or ride MAX to Hollywood and bike from there. 9-6pm, Daily 133 SW Second Ave. 503-243-2453. **MOUNTAIN SHOP**: all day rentals in the neighborhood; see page 105. **BIKETOWNPDX.COM**: Rent from and return to any orange bike share kiosk. **SPINLISTER.COM**: rent a bike from a local.

The pedestrian overpass at Northeast 42nd Avenue looked a little different in 1934. It connects the Hollywood district to the Laurelhurst neighborhood.

C

Appendix:
Selected Portland
Reference Works

Anderson, Heather Arndt. *Portland: A Food Biography.* Rowman & Littlefield, 2015

Boag, Peter. "Portland Vice Scandal (1912–1913)." www. OregonEncyclopedia.org

Bookwalter, Jack. "Mail Order Houses in Portland, Oregon." www. nwrenovation.com

Entrix, Inc. *Portland Public Schools: Historic Building Assessment,* 2009

Foster, Laura O. "Poetry on the Block: Literary Posts Abound in Portland," portlandwalking.blogspot.com, 2011

Foster, Laura O. *Portland City Walks: Twenty Explorations In and Around Town.* Timber Press, 2008

Foster, Laura O. *The Portland Stairs Book.* Timber Press, 2010

Friedman, Ralph. *In Search of Western Oregon.* Caxton Printers, Caldwell, Idaho. 1990

Gilmour, Jeff and Heather Gunderson, Doug Miller, Emily Moore and Amy Rose. "An Inquiry into Portland's Canine Quandary: Recommendations for a Citywide Off-leash Program." Portland State University, 2003

Leeson, Fred. *My-Te-Fine Merchant: Fred Meyer's Retail Revolution.* Irvington Press, 2014

MacArthur, Lewis L. and Lewis A. *Oregon Geographic Names.* Oregon Historical Society Press, 1992

Reynolds, Phyllis C. *Trees of Greater Portland.* Macrophyllum Press, 2013

Portland Bureau of Planning and Sustainability. "East Portland Historical Overview and Historic Preservation Study," March 2009

Snyder, Eugene E. *Portland Names and Neighborhoods: Their Historic Origins.* Binford & Mort, 1979

Index of Places

Index Of Places

MICROCOSM·PUBLISHING

About the Publisher

Microcosm Publishing is Portland's most diversified publishing house and distributor with a focus on the colorful, authentic, and empowering. Our books and zines have put your power in your hands since 1996, equipping readers to make positive changes in their lives and in the world around them. Microcosm emphasizes skill-building, showing hidden histories, and fostering creativity through challenging conventional publishing wisdom with books and bookettes about DIY skills, food, bicycling, gender, self-care, and social justice. What was once a distro and record label was started by Joe Biel in his bedroom and has become among the oldest independent publishing houses in Portland, OR. We are a politically moderate, centrist publisher in a world that has inched to the right for the past 80 years.

About the Author

Laura O. Foster writes about Portland and the Pacific Northwest. Her books take readers on explorations of a city or region's geology, architecture, neighborhoods, parklands, and human and natural history.

In 2009, the Hollywood Library asked Laura to create and lead walking tours to celebrate the Portland places of Beverly Cleary and the fictional kids she created—kids who skated, biked and argued on the famous Klickitat Street. For several years afterwards, Laura led the tour occasionally, for public school field trips and for OPB's *Oregon Art Beat* when it celebrated Mrs. Cleary's 100th birthday in April 2016. This book is a much expanded version of that tour.

In the 1990s Laura lived on Northeast 48th Avenue in a 1909 Craftsman bungalow, about 13 blocks from Beverly's two homes. She walked her dog to Grant Park most days with her two daughters. There, where Beverly, Henry, Beezus and Ramona played, the girls climbed trees, swung on the swings, and swam in the Grant Pool. Today Laura lives in Northwest Portland's Skyline neighborhood. Reach her on Facebook.

Other Books by Laura O. Foster

Portland Stair Walks: Explore Portland, Oregon's Public Stairs (Microcosm Publishing, 2019)

Columbia Gorge Getaways: 12 Weekend Adventures, from Towns to Trails (Towns to Trails Media, 2016)

Portland Hill Walks: 24 Explorations in Parks and Neighborhoods (Timber Press, 2005, rev. ed. 2013)

Portland City Walks: 20 Explorations in and around Town (Timber Press, 2008)

Walk There! 50 Treks in and around Portland and Vancouver (Metro, 2008, 2009)

The Portland Stairs Book : Walks, Views, Stories (Timber Press, 2010)

Lake Oswego: Images of America (Arcadia Publishing, 2009)

Boys Who Rocked the World (Co-author, Beyond Words, 2001; rev. ed. Aladdin/ Beyond Words, 2012)

Laura O. Foster at Beverly Cleary's childhood home in Yamhill, Oregon

SUBSCRIBE TO EVERYTHING WE PUBLISH!

Do you love what Microcosm publishes?

Do you want us to publish more great stuff?

Would you like to receive each new title as it's published?

Subscribe as a BFF to our new titles and we'll mail them all to you as they are released!

$10-30/mo, pay what you can afford. Include your t-shirt size and your birthday for a possible surprise!

microcosmpublishing.com/bff

...AND HELP US GROW YOUR SMALL WORLD!

...AND CHECK OUT OUR OTHER FINE GUIDES:

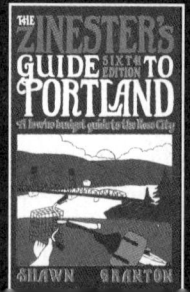

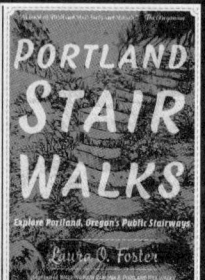